GRIEVE 2016

TRUMAN CAPOTE
A Memoir

BOOKS BY JOHN MALCOLM BRINNIN

Poems

The Garden Is Political
The Lincoln Lyrics
No Arch, No Triumph
The Sorrows of Cold Stone
The Selected Poems of John Malcolm Brinnin
Skin Diving in the Virgins

Biography

Dylan Thomas in America
The Third Rose: Gertrude Stein and Her World
Sextet: T. S. Eliot & Truman Capote & Others
Truman Capote: Dear Heart, Old Buddy

History

The Sway of the Grand Saloon: A Social
History of the North Atlantic
Beau Voyage: Life Aboard the Last Great Ships

Criticism

Emily Dickinson, *a selection of poems*
Casebook on Dylan Thomas, *a collection of essays*
William Carlos Williams, *a critical study*
Selected Plays of Gertrude Stein

Anthologies

Modern Poetry: American and British
(with Kimon Friar)
The Modern Poets: An American-British Anthology
(with Bill Read)

TRUMAN CAPOTE

A Memoir

JOHN MALCOLM BRINNIN

SIDGWICK & JACKSON
LONDON

First published in 1987 in Great Britain by
Sidgwick & Jackson Limited

Originally published in the United States of America by
Dell Publishing Co Inc

ISBN 0–283–99423–1

Printed by The Garden City Press Limited
for Sidgwick & Jackson Limited
1 Tavistock Chambers, Bloomsbury Way
London WC1A 2SG

FOREWORD

This account of a sometimes intimate association lasting nearly four decades is based on excerpts from journals I'd been keeping for years before Truman Capote stepped into them. Some entries are quoted more or less intact, others serve as touchstones to memory. In its original form, the memoir covered only the first seventeen years of Truman's adult life. Published as one of six (others were devoted to T. S. Eliot, Alice B. Toklas, Elizabeth Bowen, Henri Cartier-Bresson, and Edith Sitwell) in a book entitled *Sextet,* it took leave of him when his long labors on *In Cold Blood* were about to come to fruition— with consequences that would alter his career and check the progress of his once charmed life.

Almost twice as long as the original, this enlargement of the memoir incorporates letters discovered after the earlier version was published and—from a perspective only death could provide—recounts occasions and events that may contribute to the story of a life others will tell more objectively, but never more affectionately.

John Malcolm Brinnin

TRUMAN CAPOTE
A Memoir

At Yaddo* one June morning in 1946 I got up at dawn, worked on a poem until ten, and decided to take a sunbath. Manuscript on clipboard, I climbed a dark stairs to a door that opened to my touch like the lid of a music box. The sounds I heard came from a harplike instrument, affixed to the door's other side, which twanged a limited diapason when struck by little leaden balls hung on loose wires. Stepping out onto a crenellated terrace level with the tops of pine trees, I took off my shirt and was about to remove my pants when another twanging of the lyre told me I'd been followed—by a stranger who stood waiting for the raucous jangle to stop.

"Oh, shut up," he said. "May I join you?"

We introduced ourselves. Spelling out the letters of his last name, C-a-p-o-t-e, he said his first name was Truman. Small as a child, he looked like no other adult male I'd ever seen. His head was big and handsome, and his butterscotch hair was cut in bangs. Willowy and delicate above the waist, he was, below, as strong and chunky as a Shetland pony. He wore a white T-shirt, khaki shorts too big for him, sandals that fit as neatly as hooves.

He told me he was working on a novel, his first. He now had five chapters and a title. Did I like titles? What would I think of *Other Voices, Other Rooms*? His voice, odd and high, was full of funny

* A residence, not far from Saratoga Springs, New York, for artists—mainly writers who, upon application supported by prominent figures in their respective fields, may be invited to spend months there without cost. The largest unit of Yaddo is "the mansion"—a vast pile of Victorian brick furnished with the loot of Europe and the Middle East set among tinkling fountains in the glow of stained glass.

resonances that ran a scale of their own: meadowlark trills and, when he laughed or growled, a tugboat basso.

Before I could respond, other questions came fast: Had I read stories of his in *Harper's* and *Mademoiselle*? Had I seen his picture in *Life*? The stories, he told me, were "drawn" from dirt-road Alabama where he'd been "sort of drug up by assorted relatives." Later, he lived with his mother and stepfather in New York City and went to "this private school for kids whose fathers had weekend visiting privileges and girl friends," then Connecticut and "a high school where everyone wore saddle shoes and thought I was a creep."

"College?"

"I never set foot in one," he said. "With an IQ that runs off the chart, why should I?" He began to write "as a mere child," he said, and by the time he was sixteen had "conquered technique." This information made me stare, but I kept a straight face. Would I care to listen to a chapter?

Led into a Gothic chapel-like tower room with tall windows on three sides, I sat on something that looked like a section of a choir stall while he read from yellow foolscap in a steady, barely inflected voice that seemed suddenly to belong to another person. His respect for every one of his own nuances was contagious; I found myself listening with as much care as he took to read. With no preface to cue me in, I grasped only that a character named Joel was being put through a series of small adventures meant to test his courage and sense of reality. The story didn't matter. What did was the quality of a prose that mixed hard observations with extravagant fancy, without ever losing a grip on either. There were too many shimmering "effects" and too much poetic "atmosphere," yet his eye for detail seemed to me as exact as Faulkner's, and much less portentous, or lugubrious. Most, I was struck by his concern for rhythm; when a paragraph got off on the wrong beat, he'd stop and start over. Surprised, I said only that I'd like to hear more of it sometime.

"How about this afternoon?" he asked. "In your room—about five?"

He came at four, by which time I'd already taken a half-empty fifth of White Horse from the dresser drawer and completed my preparations: an ashtray in the shape of a lily pad, two toothbrush tumblers, Planters peanuts in a saucer kept for paper clips, a copy of Susanne Langer's *Philosophy in a New Key,* and the issue of *The Kenyon Review* with poems of mine in it—just in case conversation would lag.

It didn't. Our fellow inmates supplied more gambits than we needed. "Agnes Smedley—that woman who marched with the Red Army in China," he asked, "is she a real communist, or only a Chinese one?" Did I know that, only a few weeks ago, Katherine Anne Porter left Yaddo to stay with friends because Carson McCullers's attentions got "moony and sticky"? That the new secretary in the office—the divorcée with the wolfhound and the Buick convertible—was suspected of being an informer for the FBI? Did I know Newton Arvin?

"Only by reputation."

"You think he's an important critic . . . like Edmund Wilson?"

Yes, I told him (the sound of the dinner gong came echoing upward through the Pre-Raphaelite gloom), he *was* an important critic, "like Edmund Wilson." We started down the grand staircase to the dining room, where Truman made a beeline for the place Arvin had been keeping for him.

Late that evening I was reading Dylan Thomas when a moth with a wingspread of perhaps seven inches lighted on my desk. Astonished, I studied it for a while, calculated its small chance of life in a rude world, and captured it whole between the pages of *The World I Breathe.*

A knock at the door: Truman. Everyone else, he said, was out on the town, or working. What about me? I opened my book and showed him the expired moth.

How did it get in? he asked.

"The same way you did," I told him.

We began to spend hours together every day, avoiding the "mop-ing room" or the music room, where most of Yaddo's social life took place, in favor of sessions in the sun on his terrace or late afternoons in his sacerdotal tower or in the room—so big, bare, and sparsely furnished that it echoed—to which I'd been assigned.

He had not asked questions about Newton Arvin to satisfy an idle curiosity, I soon learned, but to hear how someone like me—more or less in the same academic game (I taught at Vassar, Arvin at Smith) —regarded him. As these questions continued, I told him that I'd seen Arvin on professional occasions, and sensed that he was both amiable and retiring. But his total bearing, I had to say, so relent-lessly caricatured the cloistered scholar as to make him a little forbid-ding. I had once met the woman from whom he was divorced, and I had read all of his books with profit. He was one of the few readers and rereaders of American literature whose insights were indispens-able. None of this made me ready to accept Truman's word that Arvin was also a man of mellow charm and wicked wit who, in a few weeks at Yaddo, had made himself irresistible, particularly to Truman.

Prepared to see Arvin with new eyes, I joined him one morning when, clerkish with gold-rimmed spectacles, he wore a dark suit to breakfast, sat like a furled umbrella, and buttered his toast to the edges. He'd been reading Melville, he said, while he made a game of pretending to himself he never had. "It's the only way," he told me, "otherwise you're apt to see the beard and the whale and the customs house and miss the man."

Amen, I said to myself.

I soon found that Truman, in a crowd or tête-à-tête, could exist on
no plane but that of intimacy—a necessity which most people did
not at first see as a compulsion but as a gift. Glad myself to accept
the gift, I began to understand the compulsion. At ease with him in
private, I could not help observing that, in public, merely by entering
a room he became a cynosure, a catalyst, the chemist's drop of vola-
tile substance that changed the composition of any gathering from
amity to effervescence. While instances of this, occurring daily, began to turn the social life of Yaddo into comedy, the journal I kept
that summer records little but glimpses of my encounter with Truman which, I thought, would end when circumstance changed.

> At home, in his tower [one journal entry reads], T.
> hands martinis to his guests—Yaddoites all, except for
> Mary Lou Aswell, an editor of *Harper's Bazaar* who's
> come from New York to see him. Then he sits in an ivory-
> colored bishop's chair holding a photograph of himself—
> the one taken in the same chair some weeks ago and
> enlarged to page size in *Life*.
> "Look," says someone at the window, "you can see
> Agnes taking down her washing." To which someone else
> adds, "She's the only woman I know who can look chic in
> combat boots—except Dietrich."
> T.'s attention is not diverted as he holds up the photo-
> graph, in turn, to Mrs. Aswell, to Newton, and to me. "I
> don't look *that* petulant, do I?"
> Since each one of us has already exchanged glances, we
> make no further comment.

> Into Saratoga with T. [reads the next day's entry], and I
> buy a raincoat. When we go on to the New Worden for a
> drink, a heavyset man in plaid shorts and a Hawaiian shirt
> who's seated at the bar swivels around, takes a long look

in our direction, and says something we don't hear. Whatever it is, everyone along the bar turns around to look us over.

"Okay, okay," says the bartender, "who's for another? I'm going off duty."

"Forget it," says Truman. "I wasn't more than fifteen years old when I decided to be so obviously who I am and what I am that anyone who so much as asked the question would look like a fool."

He comes to my room late evening and sits on the desk. "When I go home, know what I have to face up to? A back room in a Park Avenue apartment house, a view of a brick wall. If I've got a story to finish, even a letter, I have to clear the coffee table to make typewriter space. My mother's an alcoholic . . . six years now."

"Your father?"

"Joe. He adopted me when they got married. He's Cuban. He may be in Havana on business this minute. They're coming up to see me. You'll understand what I mean."

His eye falls on my leather-bound copy of John Milton.

"What's that?" he says. "Looks like a prayer book." He picks it up, opens to a page marked with a red ribbon. "You actually *read* this stuff?"

"Of course. Don't you read Flaubert?"

"That's different, unless you mean you *filch* from it."

W hen the Capotes—Joe and Nina—came for a visit, I was invited along with Newton to meet them. Frail, dark, and pretty, she seemed tense; he was outgoing, a bit brusque, anxious to please. We sat on the liturgical furniture and made conversation while Truman, edgy as a preppie on Parents' Day, stared from one window, then another.

Early evening, when the others had gone, he and I sat, lights out, to watch the rising of an enormous harvest moon on hills rolling toward Vermont.

"Well," said T., "that's my family—a bewildered woman and a man who doesn't know he's bewildered. You see why I count on friends—anyone. When my real father ran off, at least I had these aunts, these marvelous weird sisters. Then, for a long time, no one . . . until a schoolteacher. Miss Catherine R. Wood. She made me feel like an adult, we'd talk like adults, exchange books no one else ever read. She even knew who Sigrid Undset was. She wore pearls, little strings of them. She looked like the Duchess of Kent . . . at least, I thought so."

There was a tap on the door. He wiped his eyes.

"Newton," he said.

Unwilling [says my journal for July 13] to sit in the general glaze of inattention that marks any group until Truman joins it, I quit the music room after dinner, but do not escape its pall.

Speculations: Beyond his intention (not beyond his awareness) Truman has engendered in almost everyone here a heightened sense of selfhood and, merely by his presence, charged the most ordinary of occasions with imminence. Spontaneous when others are cautious, he has a child's directness, a child's indifference to propriety, and so gets to the heart of matters with an audacity strangers find outrageous, then delightful. Yet nothing he says or does accounts for the magnet somewhere in his makeup that exerts itself like a force beyond logic; he's responsible for turning the summer into a dance of bees. His slightest movements throughout the mansion, about the grounds, or on the side streets of Saratoga, are charted and signaled by sentries visible only to one another. Schemes to share his table at dinner are laid at breakfast, sometimes by single plotters, sometimes by teams united in shamelessness. There's always laughter at his table, echoing across the moat of silence in which the tables around it are sunk.

When I point this out, he sighs, says it's all too much, and makes his own schemes for privacy and avenues of escape. But his door remains wide open, and when he takes flight into Saratoga and some new hideaway, a party of familiar faces is there to welcome him.

His secret: More hungry for attention than anyone else, he's learned to bestow what he craves. For recipients, enchantment; for himself, a restless longing for a bigger audience.

Talk at the dinner table I joined next evening was polemical. Ardents all, we ignored the freshets of hilarity that came from Truman and his companions across the room and pursued the question of whether the existentialism of Camus and Sartre was, from a Marxist point of view, a cop-out, a new *trahison des clercs,* or an unexpected shot in the arm for wavering political faith. Absorbed in the argument, I felt a hand on my shoulder. "Meet you at the back door," said Truman. "We're going to the flicks—Ida Lupino. My treat, I got my check from Random House."

His treat included a stinger at the Grand Union afterward.

"Do you like Newton—*personally?*" he asked.

"Very much," I told him. "Why wouldn't I?"

"Did you know that he's one of Carson's dearest friends?" he said. "Did you know that your pal Maya Deren was a student of his? He says she talked too much. She had another name then, a Jewish name. She was supposed to be passionate about French poetry, she had all these abstract ideas—communication and the artist, crap like that. I don't think Newton understands her sort of woman."

"What sort is that?"

"Women who preach ideas, especially about art. He's more comfortable with the sickies, the ones who've lost their fathers, or ditched them . . . who make *him* their father because he's smart and old and doesn't compete."

"They sound a bit like you."

"My dear Malcolm," he said, "I *don't* think Newton's interest in Miss Carson McCullers is anything at all like his interest in me. Do I have to tell you *why?*"

> The scent of pine grows heavier [I wrote in my journal], shadows on the lawn longer. When the one phone in the mansion rings, it rings for Truman. Today his pigeon-hole at the mail desk is stuffed with business envelopes. Something's in the air, something I don't ask about.

That afternoon he told me. "One more day, I'll be sprung," he said. "I've just had a phone call . . . I'm going to New Orleans."

"Why New Orleans?"

"Cartier-Bresson. *Harper's Bazaar.* He's this photographer Mrs. Snow's imported from France. Very eminent. She wants me to do an article—impressions—to go with the pictures he's supposed to take. I used to live there, I was *born* there. Ten days, all expenses paid."

Suddenly the tower room was empty, the cabals of the breakfast table dispersed. Adrift, those of us left at Yaddo began to look for partners at Ping-Pong, Chinese checkers, croquet. Relieved of the nightly jostle for position, old friends met in an atmosphere of affectionate contempt. Truman was everywhere. To speak of him would have certified his absence. No one did.

In the course of talks in which we had mutually explored backgrounds and described friends, I had spoken to Truman of Ankey Larrabee. It was she who provided the next link in an association I had assumed was at an end when Truman took flight. "I'm back," he wrote from New York, "with, let me tell you, swollen ankles and fallen arches. But my article is finished." He went on to say that, at dinner with his friend Marguerite Young the night before, he had accepted an impromptu invitation to a party across the hall, where the first person he met was "your amazing Ankey." She was particularly sweet to him, he reported, adding that he did not find her the Gorgon I and others had somehow led him to expect. Instead, he thought her hilariously amusing, slightly wacky, "an endearingly warm girl" who, to her credit he thought, did not begin to understand that she possessed the voice of an angel and, in spite of the Egyptian deity tattooed on her wrist, the presence of a duchess.

"Did they give you my holy room after I'd gone?" he wanted to know. "Have you muffled that goofy harp? I miss you, so write me, please, and please, let us meet soon."

The next mail brought a letter from Ankey. "What do you know?" she wrote. "A Friday night séance on Greenwich Avenue and there was Truman C. I had heard several heinous things about him from the Harvard–Algonquin set, but after I had meandered through a ten-minute monologue, I came to the conclusion that no one could listen in just that way and still have the initiative to *do*. He is so *small*, though. I had a feeling he might drift helplessly away at any moment, with a stricken look backward, before oblivion quite swallowed him up. These comments, I'm afraid, are inadequate: I really thought him vastly intriguing, thoroughly simpatico, and cuddly as a Pekingese. The fact that he whispers too much, and has no sense of humor (he was horrified when I said I'd heard you'd been expelled from Yaddo for wearing a bishop's cope to dinner) adds to his pastel charm. I'll bet you ten to one he doesn't live to reach his majority. Would iron pills help?"

Truman in a state of depression was something I had not conceived of when, for the first time, I visited him at home—an apartment on upper Park Avenue so scrupulously furnished without style, reference to period, or overtures to taste, good or bad, as to define a genre. After he handed me a drink, he produced a "surprise package"—a folio of photographs, including one by Cartier-Bresson, taken in the Vieux Carré: T., in a T-shirt, seated on a wrought-iron bench under big jungle-shiny leaves, looking winsome in a slightly evil way, or slightly evil in a winsome.

"Cheer me up," he said. "I'm losing the thread."

"Of what?"

"Book, life . . . New Orleans started me thinking of things, mysterious, yet all perfectly visible. I can't get them out of my head. I sit in this apartment. *You* see it. That lamp . . . my mother. I watch her. I wonder if she remembers what *I* do, the days she'd leave me by myself in a locked room. All the time I'm hearing the heart-sick river boats you can see over the levee from Jackson Square. I'm boxed up, paralyzed. Do you think maybe there's something wrong with me that isn't just psychological?"

Even as his hands shook and his pallor made me wonder, I told him he looked all right, and tried without success to have him talk about his work with Cartier-Bresson. "How can I get in touch with Ankey Larrabee?" he asked—a question I could not answer until, a few days later, a letter from Ankey reported her new address. "I am still in poor condition from my rigadoon of a housewarming," she wrote. "Some individual (one of K.'s men, I fear) beat my head against a wall. Obviously a stranger to the group. I find, however, that concussion doesn't really keep one from the 'important' things. Yesterday I attended a garden party drinking fest at E.'s, where a lady photographer posed the company for some fly-by-night fashion magazine. Since her pictures were meant to illustrate a story proving that ordinary people now live in the Village, I was promptly trussed upon arrival, and shoved into an old cactus pot.

"There's a rumor going around the San Remo and some uptown *boîtes* that Truman C. is sick—bad sick. It sounds like leukemia. For some reason, he's not in the hospital but at home. One of these days I'm going to take him the new issue of *Screen Romances* and Cocteau's treatise on opium—illustrated—just to see if he's capable of normal responses."

Truman's subsequent letter was not reassuring. "I woke up the other day with a left foot that had the shape of a balloon," he wrote. "Infected, deeply, and for reasons that baffle both me and my doctor. I have to stay in bed, but already that has compensations: Ankey came all the way uptown to see me yesterday and we had the whole afternoon together—I propped like a pasha on my bed, she at the foot of it leaning against a blue water-silk pillow, drinking rather a lot of bourbon and eating fried chicken. A wonderful girl, Ankey, and I love her; in fact, I can't remember when I have felt so charmed and exhilarated by anyone."

A writer who had not published a book, Truman was nevertheless an "item" in the purview of New York gossip columnists and his name had a way of turning up in circles he had never entered. Some particularly sober citizens I knew—unaware that I was acquainted with him—echoed rumor and swore it was fact. Between acts the other night, he'd been seen wearing an emerald on his forehead as he chatted with his escort, Lucius Beebe. He was, as "everybody" knew, the illegitimate son of the former Chicago bus driver now known as Spencer Tracy. His family, impoverished but proud, had legally disinherited him for selling one of Robert E. Lee's dress swords to the Smithsonian. "That sore foot's a red herring," a Madison Avenue editor told me, "the kid's on his way out."

"If you're really ill," I wrote to Truman, "I ought to know about it, and from you—if only as an office of affection."

"Office of affection—balls," he wrote back. "But thank you for your sweet letter of concern. Inasmuch as I am about to enter the death house, I could not have hoped for a prettier farewell. The reason for this journey into the shadows is as follows: My red corpuscles are destroying my white ones in a process that looks like leukemia but is not, I can assure you, nearly so dangerous or as fatal. One of the sources of this ailment is, of all things, my tonsils, and they'll be zipped out. It should all be over soon. And a happier lad I'll be, for I have had to give up even the pretense of working (something which *really* makes me ill), and medical shenanigans do tend to limit one's scope.

"Speaking of fevers (which you weren't) mine's a lulu: 102 and more for two whole *weeks*. Little T.—who, bet your boots, wastes not, wants not—has of course made copious notations on the marvelous distortion of things."

He was out of the hospital within the week, and into another phase of the recurrent depression that dogged him like a nagging cold. "You are wise, dear Malcolm," he wrote, "to stay out of this city. It is no place for you, and it is unquestionably no place for me; I just can't assume the sneering facade that might help me to survive this huge snake pit; everything you say here is instantly repeated; I mean, everything you haven't said. Who are my friends and who aren't? Nothing is ever nothing; something is never something. Everything comes out quite differently from what it so innocently *is*. Kafka said it all. He would have loved New York.

"Write to me—and for the particular day of September 30, send me a greeting with forget-me-nots—or, *should* you be passing that showroom on Seventh Avenue—a little Duesenberg runabout, preferably with white-walled tires, for my birthday, that is. I'll be twenty-two."

Unable to find him on a visit to New York, or to reach him by phone, I wrote to him and learned why.

"Your letter and I arrived in New York at approximately the same time, but in rather different conditions: the letter was bright and witty and sweet, everything a letter should be, while I, on the other hand, am ill, unkempt, achy. But I had a wonderful time in Northampton. As always. Newton is very well, but very tired: those six weeks at Wesleyan were quite a strain . . . and he has so much to do, getting his Smith classes rolling, starting Melville, preparing a November lecture . . . Newton takes it all very seriously, which of course he should.

"How miserable to have missed you! And I certainly plan on seeing you Oct. 5. You may stay here in this apartment if you like (please *lower* that eyebrow), where, I assure you, you will be perfectly safe, for I am very moral these days.

"My book of stories has come to rather a halt. All terribly complicated, with cons outweighing pros at this point, even in my own mind. Still, the decision is still my own; I can if I want to, or so Random House says. But anyway I'd like to talk with you about it.

"Maya Deren paid me a little call just before I left. You knew that she is an ex-student of Newton's? He does not remember her with any pleasure. I kind of liked her though . . . that day. She is perfectly serious about these films, isn't she? And some of her ideas are interesting. I wonder, however, if she has the talent to make anything of it. I have been reading some of Garrigue's verses: Oh Malcolm, it's so awful! what merit can you possibly find? Have you ever read *Miss Lonelyhearts*? I think you would like it."

These laconic comments from the cradle were a bit much to take. My adored friend Maya Deren already seemed to me the most brilliant woman I would ever know. Jean Garrigue, confident of my admiration, had shyly entrusted me to bring her first manuscript of poems to the attention of publishers. As for Nathanael West's *Miss Lonelyhearts*, I'd read it when Truman was still making mud pies in Alabama.

A little admonitory lecture was called for, I thought, and the phone was handy.

"I got your letter," I began, "there are a few things you ought—"

"Can you come into town . . . tomorrow? I'm buried, maybe dead. Someone has to dig me up."

He'd been twenty-two for five days when, in an attempt at resurrection, I met him late afternoon in a midtown bar called Tony's Trouville. The only person there, he sat with his back against a striped wall, legs dangling, for all the world like a child dressed up who'd been told to be good and sit still.

"I tried to reach you, to call it off," he said. "I'm in the dumps."

"What's wrong?"

"The old story. I can't live where I live, can't be where I want to be. Other people go home. I have to wait for an engraved invitation from Northampton."

"Fish got to swim, birds got to fly, you mean? Can't help . . ."

"Okay," he said, "be smart . . . but that's how I am."

Mary Lou gave us dinner that night and we went on to visit Ankey on Patchin Place, where her cats, Liquid and Toynbee, showed off their pouncing act and, well trained by Miss Larrabee, bristled with electricity at the mention of e. e. cummings, who lived downstairs. Truman, miles away in her ten-foot-square living room, pretended to be amused. Finally, we dropped in at a party Maya was giving for a Rimbaud-like adolescent from France whose genius everyone suspected, but which time would not confirm. Truman, listening to the boy's broken, impressionistic English, gave him no more than flat-eyed regard. Nothing could change his mood or break his sullen silence. Since I was flying to Boston from La Guardia, we shared a taxi that dropped him off at his apartment.

"Don't give up on me," he said as the doorman stood by. "I mean, don't give me up."

"Why do you think I might?"

"It's what I always think," he said. "And I've always been right."

"As you can see," he wrote a week later, "I have changed addresses, have moved to a little lost mews in darkest Brooklyn . . .

for various reasons: I wanted most to get away from hectic, nerve-wracking influences, to escape and get on with my work. I had reached a point where I was so nervous I could hardly hold a cigarette, and my work was not going too well. So here I am living in quiet Victorian splendor in a private house belonging to two elderly, rather mad ladies; I have a charming (moderately) parlor, and a rather cheerful bedroom: I can't wait for you to see it. There is a telephone: Main 2-7070 . . . but under no circumstances are you to tell it to anyone, neither family or friends.

"Dearest Malcolm, I hope you are well. I miss seeing you, and want to so much. When you come to town next do try and save a goodly share of your time for me. And write me at once. Much love to you, darling."

Back in New York, I was having lunch with Ankey one day when she said: "Let's cross the river and track Truman down. I have this compulsion to make sure he's for real."

The late afternoon in Brooklyn was dark. Strangers helped us to find the address in a neighborhood undisturbed since the nineteenth century. Stopping at a house much like every other, we went up a musty staircase and found Truman in a room overwhelmed by wallpaper. He gave us ferocious hugs, sat us down to bourbon and Ritz crackers out of a box.

It was the first time I'd seen him and Ankey alone. Same height, they had the same flamingo-and-ivory complexion, the same butterscotch hair cut in bangs, equally dwarflike proportions and doll-like heads. The tennis shoes they wore each were gone in the left toe.

At once they entered into a cabal of their own. "When I was *your* age," said Ankey, whose age was exactly his, "I could recite all of the bridge by heart. That's a riddle."

"*His* Brooklyn wasn't this . . . his was Brooklyn Heights," Truman told her. "How do you keep the moons in your cuticles so white and clear?"

Left out of their mutual examination of belly buttons and cultural icons, I sipped my drink and cased his digs: a sepia print of the Colosseum above a disemboweled Singer; an antimacassar on a Morris chair; Andalusian draperies with tassels; ghostly cabbage roses on a threadbare carpet. The only things in sight conceivably his were a record player, a black-and-gold ashtray from the Rainbow Room, books (among them Newton Arvin's *Whitman*), a portable Olivetti in its case, a photograph of himself, and the Webster's Unabridged against which it was propped.

"Don't you get to feeling sort of buried over here, Truman?" I asked.

"Of course," he said, "that's why I'm here. No-man's-land. Ask a cabdriver to take you somewhere, he has to look at a map. It's not just Brooklyn they're lost in, they're lost in 1946. This cruddy hotel where I get dinner . . . for the people who live there, everything turns on what radio program, how many scoops of ice cream, who had a maid and maybe a Persian-lamb coat with mink cuffs in 1922. My landlady thinks the Jews are poisoning the water system. Her brother still writes to Father Coughlin. The subway's literally abysmal, but it's like crossing the border and you can make the trip both ways any day in the week."

"I went to Staten Island once," said Ankey. "It was like Australia."

Brooklyn had provided Truman with a place to work, and with problems unforeseen. Less than two months into his self-imposed exile, loneliness and a recognition of how "the ordinary demands of daily living can devour a person body and soul" had brought him to despair. "How can I ever clear away these mountains of obstructions," he wrote, "and get on with what I have to do? Histrionic as it must sound, I wonder whether I shall indeed survive the winter; everything I do turns against me. It is simply harrowing now for me to be alone; there is so little I can do for myself. And there is no one to turn to, really no one. All of my friends are of course wonderful and, I know, would do most anything asked of them. Unfortunately, this does not bring relief or alter the circumstance."

With the relief of weekends in Northampton and frequent return visits to his parents' roof, he did indeed survive the winter. But one problem that had at first seemed an annoyance had developed into a persistent worry: How was he going to join his professional life with his emotional life? What modus vivendi was possible for the gregarious young artist and the cloistered scholar? As much a bird out of habitat in Northampton as Newton Arvin was in Manhattan, Truman was nevertheless the one more free to come and go, and so he did. But from what I detected in phone talks with him, his campus visits were always briefer than he wished, and Newton's sojourns in New York had a way of being cut short by real, or convenient, demands for his early return to academe.

I'd not seen Truman for months when, one evening early in February, I saw Arvin. The point of this occasion was Newton's contribution to an article on the nature of the postwar college generation that I'd been commissioned to do, but the substance of the interview was, inevitably, Truman.

At the depot, as my train from Boston pulled in, Newton was wearing neat ankle-high boots, a close-fitting gray overcoat, a felt hat protected by a plastic covering. Through high-piled banks of snow we walked up the hill to Rahar's for a quick dinner and then went on to his place, an attic apartment in a big frame house. Spare, tidy, and anonymous, it had the uninhabited and slightly forlorn air of a furniture show-window at night.

"Truman's found a solution," he said as he placed his boots outside the entrance, "perhaps a necessary one. . . . Those rooms in Brooklyn. *He* thinks he's escaping confinement. *I* think he's gone back to Alabama and his tree house. You've seen the place, you gather my meaning . . . back to all the shabby little icons of gentility he pretends to despise, to the kind of people he used to know . . . lives obsessed by trivia and simplified by bigotry."

Bringing me ice cubes in a glass, he handed me a pint bottle of Scotch. "But there's a difference, of course," he continued. "That big world he used to sight through the branches is no longer a dream. For the price of a subway fare he can enter it and leave it. He needs both, I suppose—Turgenev and Flaubert to intrigue the artist part of his nature on Thursday night, El Morocco and café society to let him play the boulevardier on Saturday. An odd balance, you might say. But as long as he lives, I think he'll try to maintain it."

Over his shoulder, matted and framed, Cartier-Bresson's photograph of Truman in New Orleans made its ambiguous invitation.

"You know that he's been up here with me several times." He motioned toward a window where a streetlamp shone through high branches outlined with snow. "Who knows? Perhaps this is still another tree house. I can't tell whether he's happy here or not. But he comes back . . . he comes back."

In New York to keep a dinner date with Truman a week later, I spent the afternoon at the Museum of Modern Art's double show: Henry Moore and Cartier-Bresson. Looking first at the sculptures, I found myself unexpectedly moved by the way in which Moore, indulging himself in the grotesque, invoked the serene. The photographs, by contrast, seemed to me seductive and larcenous, shaming the eyes they attracted. Both exhilarated and disturbed by the experience, I went uptown to Truman's and found him alone, listening to a murky recording of early jazz.

"What," he asked, "is a Hartford Wit?"

"You doing a crossword puzzle?"

"I just want to *know*," he said.

I told him.

"Well," he said, "at least that makes a little sense. These young men keep turning up at Newton's with dissertations—is that what I mean, dissertations?—in the glove compartments of their Studebakers. One of them came up from Yale with this five-hundred-page manuscript on the Hartford Wits. Just the idea baffles me. I think about him. You and I are having dinner at Schrafft's."

"Why Schrafft's?"

"Because," he said with a sort of emphatic demureness, "I have reason to remain incognito."

My task, when I'd said good-bye to Truman that evening, was to pick up a painting given to me by Theodoros Stamos as a reward for having supplied titles for the works in his recent show. When I got to his studio, Stamos was wrapping it, a process that took so long that, when I'd lugged the painting to Grand Central, I found I'd missed the last train to Poughkeepsie. When the painting wouldn't fit into any of the twenty-five-cent lockers, I took it back to Truman's for the night.

Asleep in his guest bed, I was soon awake.

"Malcolm," Truman was saying, "what exactly do academic people mean by a sense of evil? Newton says Hawthorne had it and Melville had it, and he thinks I do. Does it mean believing, really believing, in something like the devil? Or does it just mean that you can see that there's something terribly wrong with God and the universe and say so? Do *you* think I have a sense of evil?"

"Djuna Barnes speaks of 'the mad strip of the inappropriate that runs through creation.'"

"That," he said, "I can understand."

In the course of his collaboration with Henri Cartier-Bresson on the New Orleans story, Truman had spoken of me to the eminent photographer and had later arranged for us to meet. In the seven months since that event, Cartier-Bresson and I had become friends and were about to become working partners on a transcontinental trip for which we had obtained a publisher's commission. Happy to tell Truman about this development, I found him as, just back from another visit to Northampton, he waited for me at the Algonquin.

"The happiest weekend ever," he said, and took from his wallet a snapshot of Newton: a smiling middle-aged man whose gold rims now seemed to glint with a touch of the roué.

"I think I'm developing a little taste for the life you academics lead," said Truman. "We went to dinner with the president of the college and some of the faculty one evening—a completely civilized occasion, I thought, and we had lunches with some types—*you* know, pipes that won't stay lit, ribbon ties, suede patches on J. Press elbows? One of them was working on Bronson Alcott, another on someone called Joaquin Miller. They must have wondered what *this* one was doing there. But they were absolutely sweet to me. Newton wants to ask you something. You'll say I put him up to it, but I didn't."

"What does he want to ask?"

"It's this: We're thinking of Nantucket for the summer, but Newton has this conviction that I'd be overwhelming to live with. Even when I'm being a perfect mouse, reading in a corner of the room somewhere, he says I'm overwhelming. He'll be on his Melville, with luck I'll write finis to *Voices*. Would you consider sharing a house with us there?"

"To save Newton Arvin from being swamped by the likes of you?"

He gave me a scrutinizing, possibly angry, look. "We're trying," he said, "to be realistic."

On the road with Cartier-Bresson, I would not see Truman again for nearly five months. When the end of the transcontinental journey was in sight, I wrote to tell him I'd soon be within range, and received his reply in Boston: "How pleasant to have your note from the Smoky City and even more pleasant to know that you are, or rather were, so near the end of your junket; I sympathized with you every *step* of the way, and envied you too: isn't it marvelous the *sudden* things you see while working with a photographer, more particularly a photographer like Henri? Naturally, I am frantically anxious to hear all the details—which brings me to a point: if you can come for a visit, and heaven knows I want you to, I rather wish you could make it late in August. In fact, I shall be absolutely *alone* from Sept. 1st until the 15th. Does the space between those dates appeal to you? Before that, however, the situation is exceedingly complicated. Newton will be here until August and he is working hard on his book, and Isherwood is coming on the 10th, to be followed by Mary Lou and her brood."

The livelier part of the letter suggested that his life and letters had come into a harmony ("I am as happy as I ever thought I could be") which I'd begun to think he would never find.

"This comes from a desk at which I can hear, if not see, the arriving surf (how's that for taming an intransitive verb?) and when you are reading this I'll have crossed the last 't' of my book—which I'm anxious for you to read *in toto*. O, dear, what a long slow struggle. But it's done—and so am I, to a turn, I mean—ever so golden, and all over, too; for there are heavenly stretches of sand here where one can go trunkless.

"Speaking of things to see, have you turned your John the Baptist gaze on my unutterably awful photo in the current "entertainment" rag? Never again, I swear. What a travesty!

"Boston: Newton took me there last week, my first visit ever, and I loved it—for such diverse experiences as dinner with F. O. Matthiessen and a marvelously tacky show at the Old Howard (I'm an old burleycue buff, you'll remember). Matthiessen I did not especially take to; only someone like Proust could tell me why—so I will have to wait until someone like that comes along. Harry Levin I *did* like

—even though I felt I must be the sort of person who tunes him tight as a drum.

"Now that I'm really, *really* writing finis to my book, I'm not so much relieved, as you might think, as angry. The strain to finish it in time for what the publishers consider D day has been intolerable and I'm convinced in my heart that it is a failure. Jesus. It strikes me (but what does it matter now?) that I've been forced into a sort of competition with myself and that's not fair. O dear, so *what?*"

With doubts he had kept to himself, Truman had promoted my acquaintance with Cartier-Bresson and encouraged my collaboration with him. When the collaboration and the relationship came into trouble, it was Truman who, by accident, confirmed the deceit that undermined and ended both.

In the course of a transcontinental trip by car lasting from mid-April through July, Cartier-Bresson took thousands of photographs, while I made hundreds of pages of notes. The idea was to combine visual documentation by an alien and social commentary by a native in a book based on a grand tour in which, in Cartier's words, we would be *"les flâneurs des deux océans."*

At the moment of our setting out, contracts for this volume were being drawn up and were to be forwarded to us en route. On our very first day on the road, my collaborator casually informed me that he had unilaterally put aside contractual security in order, he said, to be "free," to allow us to "do all ways what we like." This from an artist of Henri's stature seemed reasonable in its bid for unhampered creativity. On any other terms—professional, affectionate, or just plain human—his brusque cancellation of a contract we'd spent months in pursuing was sufficiently puzzling to send a little frisson of uneasiness across my line of sight. But we were on our way, after all, and private doubts had no place in an undertaking so challenging and exhilarating.

At its conclusion, I first used my notes to identify Cartier's contact prints and put them in sequence, then to pinpoint the themes and motifs of a conversation lasting nearly three months. My tasks had just been completed when, one afternoon early in September, I joined Cartier at his New York apartment. There he handed me a mock-up, a sequence of photographs, roughly joined and crudely bound, which nevertheless had the appearance of a book.

"A presentation to publishers," he said. "By turning pages, they can see what has been done."

Turning pages, so could I: From thousands upon thousands of photographs, he had chosen exactly one hundred and ten. A third or more of these had been taken on the streets of Manhattan during the previous winter. The other sixty-five or seventy, taken together, constituted a study in morbidity amounting to a pathological casebook: deformed or otherwise gross figures, some of whom looked back in alarm or hostility at the man who had stalked them; others of whom, cornered by the camera, were too lethargic to care or too visibly cretinous to comprehend. The blue cardboard binding carried no title, only neatly drawn letters, "Foreword by Cartier-Bresson." Leafing through the collection twice, I put it aside and waited for the joke to be explained.

"Eli is preparing some nice tea, from Singapore," said Henri. "Friends will be coming. I have promised you will read those excellent pages we have heard in Saratoga."

His wife entered with a tray. "So long now we do not see you, Chon," she said. "Many times Henri says, 'Without Chon I am one without arms. I see this thing I do not understand, I turn to inquire, Chon is not there . . . I am like his twin, missing.' "

Among the several friends they'd asked in was Truman. I read for half an hour, uncomfortably aware that my words had only the vaguest and most incidental pertinence to the photographs they were meant to accompany. As I concluded, there was a smatter of handclapping and an approving murmur. Eli spoke to Truman. "It's true, no? Like those words you have already said about New Orleans?"

He poked me. "Let's cut this short," he said.

Out in the street, he suggested we have dinner "somewhere different." Since my car was parked nearby, I proposed we drive to a place I knew up the Hudson—the Lake Tavern, in Ardsley. Across town and onto the West Side Highway, I mulled thoughts that eluded conclusions. We drove in silence until Truman asked me what I "made" of the mock-up.

As much puzzled as affronted by Cartier's curious selection, I said no more than that I found it trivial and bizarre.

"That's about what I think," said T. "Where's there any room for what *you* have to say?"

The place for that, I told him, was with the pictures we took from the sand dunes of Cape Cod to the ledges of Big Sur, with the thousands of shots I had labeled and put in sequence.

The sun dropped behind the Palisades. We curved around Mohonk Circle and continued northward.

"Malcolm," said Truman, "are you quite certain in your mind and heart that there's ever going to *be* a text?"

He lit a cigarette, stared into the evergreen twilight on one of Westchester's little lakes.

"I hate to tell you this . . ." he said and, at length, did. "This" turned out to be a visit by Christopher Isherwood to the Cartier-Bresson flat, during which Henri's mock-up was passed around for comment. Intrigued by the coincidence, Truman had asked Christopher if he'd also had a chance to look at some of the text—only to be told that there was no text, except for the foreword. But, said Truman, he knew for a fact that there was going to be a text because he was acquainted with the person Cartier had commissioned to write it. Not *this* book, said Isherwood, perhaps some other book.

I kept my eyes on the road, dark enough now for headlights. "Why did you wait so long to tell me?"

"I couldn't believe it."

"Do you now?"

"In my considered opinion, Cartier will never allow anyone to be identified with his holy pictures but himself," he said. "If I can draw my conclusions, it's high time you drew yours."

Conclusions evaded me, but speculation was less pusillanimous: Could it be that, in his agent's files and available at a price, Cartier's photographs were worth, item by item, incomparably more than they would be worth published between covers, text or no text? I wrote him a letter reflecting this turn of thought and, hungry for corroboration, showed it to Truman.

"Nothing else makes sense," he said. "Put it in the box."

This was not the first instance in which Truman's analytical clarity about the way people operated had impressed me. But it was the one in which, for the first time, I felt that my vaguely avuncular role in his life had undergone a change amounting almost to a reversal. The idea that Truman might come to be my Dutch uncle was outrageous. Yet, for many years to come, this would be increasingly the case.

Meanwhile, I tried to maintain, if no longer to protect, the aura of éminence grise with which he had endowed me and to pretend to a degree of wisdom I could not in my heart claim. My journal entries at this time tell me only that I frequently saw Truman, or talked with him by phone. Most of these are bare notations stating when and where, but some of them—like the evening we spent with my old friend Bowden Broadwater and his bride, Mary McCarthy—are attempts to capture an occasion in some detail:

> 10.6.47 New York. Dinner with T. Afterward, dawdling along Fifty-seventh Street, we are about to pass the Broadwaters' entryway when I suggest we pay a call.

"Would Mary McCarthy like me?" he says. "She frightens me."

"She's not as scary as people make out," I tell him, "of course she'll like you."

"I have the impression she hates everybody."

"She hates Stalinists and bad style. You don't fit."

I locate the nameplate and bell button, lift my index finger. "Well?"

"Oh—why not," he says. "She can't *eat* me."

Our timing is bad. Mary is clearing plates of artichoke debris to make room for the steak, sizzling on a grill, which she is about to serve to their guests—Delmore Schwartz and Wayne Andrews. I apologize, suggest we find another occasion. Mary insists we stay.

Supplied with Scotch and soda, T. and I sit on the edge of the meal and remain for the evening. In the course of it, Delmore, who knows I've spent the late summer at Yaddo, backs me into a corner.

"Caligula Lowell still wandering the woods buck naked," he says, "passing out over Vergil and Kentucky bourbon?"

"Not with Roethke around," I tell him. "They keep close tabs on one another."

"I got the picture from Isaac Rosenfeld," he says. "Which one of them's headed for the funny farm first?"

"Come off it, they're as sane as you are."

"Poor guys," says Delmore.

Truman is seated between Mary and Bowden and, I expect, caught in the sort of Nick and Nora crossfire they tend to indulge in when they have an audience, perhaps even when they don't. I keep an eye out for a sign from him that we should be moving on.

Delmore comes back at me: "I hear you've been seeing a lot of my ex-wife."

Not lately, I tell him, adding that I was about to ask him where she is.

"Simple," he says, "find out where Lowell is."

"I *know* where Lowell is."

The look he gives me is steely. "Haven't I told you what you want to know?"

There's a chime of laughter from across the room. Truman, accepting another drink, wriggles back into his chair. The lamb has lain down with the lioness. We stay on. . . .

But not, as I learned a few days later, in the midst of that peaceable kingdom I had supposed.

"It's funny about McCarthy and Bowden," wrote Truman, "but I keep thinking about that evening. They are obviously people you like, but are you oblivious to the fact that they have no more in common with you than cats with a canary? They stand for all of the things in this world I most dislike. If only they'd cut the comedy and allow themselves a modicum of honesty. How can such brainy individuals continue to be so self-deceived, so eager to ride herd on everyone who's dared to do anything that doesn't meet with their exquisite approval? I am afraid they are members of that ever-increasing tribe—the coldhearted ones. Exclude feelings and emotions as they do and you just have to die a little inside yourself, every day. Mary, of course, has certain demonstrated talents, unhealthy though they may be. . . ."

We met next at his place in New York. "Brooklyn," he said, "I'm through with it . . . a little episode that became a bad joke. I've spent all day recovering."

"From what?—moving?"

"Nothing *quite* so plebeian. A hangover, torn ligaments. I was out until three A.M. with Mister John Gielgud. He taught me how to do the rumba," he said, and handed me a bundle of page proofs. "Read them as if you'd never heard of me. Then cross your heart, hope to die, and say what you think."

Other Voices, Other Rooms, I discovered, was a dream I could interpret. Everything Truman had told me was there—in translation, in disguise, yet unmistakably. Not expecting so strict a roman à clef, I could guess identities, reconstruct metaphors, match motive and clue as though the novel were a detective story the outcome of which I already knew.

When I took the proofs back to him one night, I found only his parents. "Truman's out to a show," said his father, "come on in, glad to see you." Accepting the proofs, he put them aside, leaving me uneasily aware that I'd never before been in his parents' company when Truman wasn't present.

"You know that friend of Truman's," asked his father, "the professor?"

"Newton Arvin."

"Fine man," he said, "like you, good for the boy. His mother here thinks the same way, she knows what I mean."

He turned to his wife. "Right, Nina?"

Smiling privately, she seemed to be on the edge of sleep.

"You come, glad to see you," he said. "Come any time, glad to see you. We get some funny customers, I tell you. Know what I mean?"

Not quite sure that I did, I said, "I do."

"This book he's been carrying around for how many years now. Suppose it don't add up? How's he going to pay the rent, feed the kitty?"

The book, I told him, would "add up," that there was no cause for worry.

"You think *so?* Nina, you hear?"

But he spoke only to a door still swinging from his wife's passage as, empty glass in hand, she returned to the kitchen.

"I got that problem, too," he said. "How about a cigar?"

When my five years at Vassar College came to an end in 1947, I rented a house in Weston, Connecticut. There, from a shipshape little room that reminded me of a cabin on the *Queen Mary,* I meant to sail into a career cleanly divided between teaching assignments in Missouri and California I had already accepted and books for which I had signed contracts. As it turned out, I would soon learn that the weather above a pond in Connecticut could be as rough as on the open ocean.

There one brilliant morning in December, I was studying the movements of a pheasant in the sedges of that pond when the phone rang.

"Three guesses," said Truman. "I've got an invitation, a commission. It involves travel."

"Atlantic City? Niagara Falls? Two weeks at Mammoth Cave, all expenses paid?"

"Very funny," he said, "you could be a comedian. But you're right about one thing—carte blanche. I'm off to Hollywood, to do a story for *Vogue* any way I want. I may not come back."

I spent the Christmas holidays in Bermuda and, my journal tells me, extended my stay until "1.9.48."

> The flying boat (you sit face-to-face in a compartment, as on a European train) splashes down in Baltimore. I take the first train north and phone Truman when I get to Penn Station.
>
> "Where've you been?" he says. "Why weren't you here to welcome me back? Can you come over . . . this minute?"
>
> I find him in a haze of cigarette smoke, a litter of butts, newspapers, cups dark with coffee dregs. In black pants, nubbly sweater, Capezios, he's pallid and thin.

"The place probably looks like some kind of hideout," he says.

"What's the matter?"

"I don't know." He wipes his right eye with the palm of his hand. "Everything. I can't sleep. One endless hangover, days, weeks."

"Since you got back?"

"Before . . . even in Hollywood. I've been living on cereal and instant coffee."

"Joe and Nina?"

"They're in Cuba." He reaches down and from the side of the couch produces a fifth of Old Grand-dad. "You like some of this?"

"Not now."

"Do you realize that my book's coming out in ten days?" he says. "From what I've been told, the reviews are going to turn my stomach."

He pours a drink into a cup. His hand, dark with nicotine, is trembling.

"Know something, Truman? You're coming home with me."

"Don't be silly. I can't even make my way to Lexington Avenue." He sips his drink, stares at the floor.

"How far *is* Weston?" he says.

I pack a bag I find in a bedroom closet, bundle him into an overcoat. Out on the sidewalk, he stands shivering like a puppy in a blanket. The doorman's whistle brings a cab.

My car's where I left it, in a lot near the Westport railroad station, banked with snow. Truman helps me scrape the windshield and rear window. Into Westport like a float in an ice carnival, we stop for a blue plate special at the greasy spoon on main street. Leaving him there over coffee, I make a quick trip to a grocery store.

The road out of town is a frosty tunnel. My uphill

driveway has been obliterated by drifts and smoothed over. We abandon the car and drag luggage and paper bags as we stump, knee-deep, up to the house. There we have to dig with our hands to make a space big enough for the storm door to swing open. Stamping ourselves dry, we begin to thaw out in the warmth of a log fire, Courvoisier, Bessie Smith on the turntable. On a couch by the fireplace, Truman lies flat as a mummy and is soon asleep. I put a blanket over him and leave him there.

1.10.48 New-fallen snow on snow. We're more snow-bound than ever. Truman, glazed, sits on a kitchen stool watching me squeeze orange juice and fry eggs.

To get him out of Hollywood, I start him talking about it—a ploy that works. By noon, when the mutters and rumblings of the furnace have punctuated a reel of reminiscence in which Charlie and Oona, Kate and Bette and Joan have all come in for close-ups and fade-outs, he seems almost himself again.

Outside, a hushed grayness, another heavy sky waiting to spill. We open cartons and cans, stare from the windows, speak when we feel like speaking.

"What if everyone hates the book?" he says. "Those thugs that wait for people like me—that pack of wolves around the *Partisan*. What if they decide to gang up? What defense do you have against reviews anyway?"

Poets, I remind him, are lucky even to *get* reviewed.

"But," he says, "what if someone sets out to demolish you? I have it on impeccable authority there's one review so vicious the editors have refused to print it."

"Who told you that?"

"A kind friend, ho ho. But I believe him."

We play gin rummy; feed carrots to a pony that turns up at the back door; take turns reading S. J. Perelman aloud; listen to Wanda Landowska; make a salmon soufflé.

The radio says snow is general over southern New England; small craft warnings are up from Eastport to Block Island.

1.11.48   A car with chains makes it halfway up the drive: Barney C. with eggs and the Sunday papers. No reviews of *Other Voices,* but big splashy full-page advertisements: THIS IS TRUMAN CAPOTE in huge type under a photograph of T. reclining in his waistcoat. Sloe-eyed, looking out from beneath his baby bangs with a sort of insouciant challenge, he has one hand prettily "disposed," as in some plaster piece of kitsch sculpture. I tear out the page, thumbtack it to the edge of the mantel.

"Why did you do that?" he asks.

"I want to think, speculate—on what I'd be apt to say if I'd never laid eyes on you."

He stares. I stare.

"Well?"

"I don't know. Do you *want* to look like the last pressed flower in *The Yellow Book?*"

"What's that?" he says.

1.12.48   The glittering crust surrounding the house looks solid but isn't. On our way to the car, I sink to my knees, Truman to his waist, and his suitcase tumbles open. At the foot of the hill, he stops to look back. "Good-bye, little house," he calls into the stillness, "don't forget me, little house."

By the time we've dug the car out, the sun is high. We drive through snowshine and long blue shadows to the depot. Waiting for his train to pull out, I spot him framed in a frosty window and lift my hand. He makes fish mouths through the pane, saying something that makes him smile.

Back at the house, I park in the road, reach the door by

stepping in the tracks we've just made. The fire has gone out. The page torn from the *Herald Tribune* hangs from the mantelpiece.

1.18.48 Sunday breakfast in Harvard Square. At the adjoining table, young husband in Eisenhower jacket and chinos, young wife in peasant blouse and dirndl, their infant in a high chair. They pass sections of *The New York Times* between them, now and then turning to spoon something to the baby.

"Take a look at this," says the husband, and holds up an advertisement showing the book jacket photograph of Truman supine in his calculated languor.

The wife gives it one stiff, stern glance.

"Honey," she says, *"you* stay away from *him."*

The baby gurgles.

"Precisely what I predicted," said Truman on the phone next day. "The knives are flashing."

"What knives?"

"The *Times,* Sunday after next. They're going to slice me paper thin."

"What about the *Trib?"*

"A rave. But what good is that? Who reads the *Herald Tribune* anymore?"

"Time?"

"I hear it's snotty."

"Well, at least it's coverage. . . ."

"Coverage! I've had more of that than the Virgin Mary."

Coverage, indeed. Two weeks later, when I got to Missouri to begin a term as poet-in-residence at Stephens College, an item in the *St. Louis Post-Dispatch* suggested that news of Truman's debut had matched that of the President's decline:

To the Editors,

Your newspaper seems to be full of two things these days—Truman Capote and Truman kaput.

Art Reiss, Leesburg, Mo.

Truman went to Haiti while I was in Missouri, but not before we'd made plans for dinner when we'd both be back in New York at the end of February. On the appointed date, thunderstorms over Ohio forced my plane to make an emergency landing in Dayton and it was well after nine when, hurrying into the lobby of the Algonquin, I found him autographing a copy of his book for a tall young man wearing a Wallace for President button.

"How's the Bible Belt?" he said.

"How was Haiti?" I asked as we were shown to the table he'd reserved.

"Almost died," he said. "Some kind of jungle fever so baffling it scared the doctors. And I don't mean the witch doctors. I couldn't tell if the drums and chants I heard were up in the hills somewhere or in my head. I'd ask the nurses but they'd never say because they never understood what I was talking about. Then I convinced myself they weren't nurses at all, simply some quiet girls who'd been told to stay with me until I'd closed my eyes for the last time. Then I gave up and went into these long jags of weeping. . . .

"Wolcott Gibbs," he said as he waved a hand across the room. "I got to know him when I was a sort of glorified office boy at *The New Yorker.* Used to be a sourpuss . . . now it turns out he's crazy about my book. Look, would you drop me off on your way? I have an appointment—on Gramercy Park. . . .

"As I was saying, I learned something—all those tears and sobs weren't just for me. I mean, I think I understood for the first time in my life that I wasn't nearly as interested in saving my *skin* as in saving what I *know,* stories I've got to tell. The thought that I'd never have the chance to tell them was worse than the idea of death itself. Oh . . . maybe everyone has stories to tell. What I mean is, I have something to say that hasn't been said, simply because no one else knows what I know in the *way* I know it."

A waiter, conspicuously hovering, reminded us that it was after midnight.

"Would you believe me if I told you I'd had a letter from Ernest Hemingway?"

"Why shouldn't I?"

"Because it's not the kind of letter you'd think."

"Well, what kind is it?"

"A denunciation, a diatribe, out of the blue. I can't figure out if he was plastered at the time or if he'd momentarily gone off his head, can't understand why he wrote it at all."

"What's his point?"

"If there *is* a point, it's a warning to keep off his turf. Cuckoo as that sounds, it's the only explanation. A lot of people are put off by the publicity the book's been getting, but at least they know there's a *book*. Hemingway goes straight for *me.*"

"You sure it's not a hoax?"

"From Finca Vigia, San Francisco de Paula? Who else would go to the trouble?"

The waiter put down our check. "My treat," said Truman, "I'd pay a lot more to a psychiatrist."

I retrieved my suitcase and we got into a cab.

"Who," I asked, "is on Gramercy Park?"

"A new friend."

"?"

"You'd call him John, everyone else calls him Julie. He's here on location, making a picture. It sounds god-awful: *Skipper Next to God.*"

"Are you talking about John Garfield?"

"I'm as surprised as you are," he said. "After all, he's still Mister Tough Guy to most of the American population."

Our taxi pulled up before a tall house.

"I've got keys," said Truman. "God knows how long I'll have to wait. But at least there's a good record collection."

Driving off, I wondered what to believe. Was this but another episode in the story of a sissy kid from the sticks who now sees himself as the *garçon fatal* of the western world? Months ago, he'd quite casually made reference to the "congenial" night he'd spent with Errol Flynn. What bothered me was that the encounter with Flynn was also supposed to have taken place in a Gramercy Park apartment. Reluctant to be the dupe of his macho fantasies, a few days later I bore down.

"This thing between you and Golden Boy," I asked. "How serious is it?"

"He's sweet . . . and sort of teddy bear cuddly, that's all. He may not be one of your towering intellects, but he's sensitive in a smoldery sort of way, and he laughs in the right places. What more does anyone need?"

My silence was inconclusive.

"What I can't stand is, he treats me like a girl."

"What does that mean?"

"It means . . . well, he's like all those others who can't face up to the fact they're with a man with balls as hairy as their own and so they have to pretend this man they're with is really some baby doll in disguise."

Our next meeting was coincidental. Invited by our mutual friend the editor Leo Lerman to one of his Sunday night "at homes," I entered a room where five hundred people, or perhaps no more than a hundred, obscured the walls, the furniture, the wine supply, and one another. Shuffling into the multitude, I was stopped by a shout: "Malcolm!"

The crowd I'd joined parted before me like the Red Sea, to make a passageway across the length of the room. At the end of it stood a figure in velvet pants, dancing pumps, a turtleneck sweater over which, on a chain of silver, dangled a medallion as big as a saucer: Truman. Sprinting toward me, he gave me an ascending series of hugs of such vigor, I felt as though I were being climbed.

"Like my outfit?" he said. "Julie was supposed to be here."

Flustered and off-base, I edged toward the wine table and was interrupted by Aline Bernstein, tugging at my sleeve. In her other hand she held a glass of something that looked like Scotch.

"Where did you get that?" I asked.

One finger at her lips, she said, "Come."

We inched into a bedroom. Fishing in the pocket of a coat on one of the beds, she produced a pint bottle of Haig & Haig.

"Doctor's orders," she said. "I'm on a diet—steak and this. Find a cup and help yourself."

A large-boned man with snowy hair poked his head in.

"Carlo!" said Aline, and gave him a kiss. "You two know each other?"

"You're the man who wrote 'Little Elegy for Gertrude Stein,'" said Carl Van Vechten as we shook hands. "I'm the man who scissored it out of *Harper's* and sent it to Alice Toklas."

"I'd wondered," I told him. "In her letter about it she said only that she had it from a friend, someone she didn't name."

"I must say you got a warm greeting from Truman," he said. His grin contained a hint of benediction. "So you're the famous professor from Smith?"

"John's at Vassar," said Aline. "We ride the local to Poughkeepsie together."

"Excuse *me*," said Van Vechten.

Between planes at La Guardia a month later, I phoned Truman at his apartment.

"I'm alone," he said, "could you stay over for a night?"

Canceling my plane, I found him in his working clothes: corduroys, white shirt, an open vest; and he was wearing horn-rimmed glasses.

"Why the specs?"

"I like to play with them," he said. "The awful truth is I need them. Sit down, I'll tell you some sad stories. A martini?"

"You know any certified paranoids?" he called from the kitchen.

"One certified," I called back, "half a dozen who haven't achieved clinical status."

Handing me a glass, he said, "I'm beginning to feel funny about a lot of things and I'm not sure of the symptoms."

"Be philosophical, like Delmore Schwartz. 'Just because I'm paranoid,' he says, 'doesn't mean everyone isn't against me.' "

"Be serious," said Truman. "I have to get out of this city, permanently. I used to be sure of a few things. Now I'm not. Why these personal attacks? I don't just mean Hemingway, I mean all these dealers in innuendo, as if I were spreading germs. Why don't they look at my *book*, say what they think about that . . . instead of digging their claws into me?"

"You're being naïve," I told him. "Haven't you encouraged that kind of reaction, even asked for it?"

"How have I asked for it?"

"That jacket photograph, to start with. . . ."

"It's sold a lot of copies, hasn't it? Been printed in every paper from here to Salt Lake City, hasn't it? I mean something else, and I'm not the only one."

He handed me a clipping out of a recent issue of *Horizon*—an excerpt from an editorial by its editor, Cyril Connolly. " 'Get Capote,' " it read. "At this minute the words are resounding on many a sixtieth floor and 'get him' of course means make him and break him, smother him with laurels and then vent on him the obscure hatred which is inherent in the notion of another's superiority."

Next morning, rummaging for breakfast, I shut the refrigerator and turned to find Truman in his bathrobe at the kitchen table.

"Last night," I asked, "were you being totally honest? Or were you fishing for something?"

He looked up, eyes wide. "Honest about what?"

"Your big show of anguish, why there's so much more gossip about you than serious attention to your book. *You* read the columns. Who's to separate that kind of chaff from the truth?"

"Some of that chaff *is* the truth," he said. "What kind of truth do *you* mean?"

"The simple fact that you work harder and longer than anyone else in the game."

"So?"

"To stringers on a butterfly chase, that's a pretty dreary piece of information. But why keep it out of sight if you're only going to suffer the consequences you say you do?"

"Don't you fret," he said. "This kid knows how to skin his own cat."

He dropped a slice of bread into the toaster. "I'm making a declaration of independence, I'm going to Paris."

"Why Paris?"

"My book's succès fou there, they tell me, why shouldn't *I* be?" The teakettle shrieked.

"Actually," he said, "I hate to go, because of Newton."

"Then why do it?"

"All I can say is, there are certain limits to what one can endure."

I drove to California in 1948 and spent the summer in Berkeley, lecturing to classes so crowded and sprawling they seemed like political rallies. While there, I got letters from Paris—not from Truman but from other friends whose reports confirmed Truman's notion that he was the victim of some intangible conspiracy of malediction. Its nature, as far as I could see, was gratuitous, and its claims could sometimes be ascribed to envy. Still, the consistent disparagement of Truman by people I had believed normally charitable began to trouble me as, thrust and parry, I found myself uneasily engaged in the defense of a friend who needed none.

Both of us were back in New York by September when, one evening, we were sitting at a window table in the rooftop bar of the Beekman Towers Hotel.

"Gide gave me this ring," said Truman and held out his hand. "It's sapphire. Cocteau made me a costume, fresh laurel leaves and a mousseline toga—and took me to a party. One day I went to see Colette, tea for two, in a boudoir that smelled of sachet and cat pee. Cocteau said she'd never heard of me, but when he told her I looked ten years old and had a mind as wicked as Egypt, she got interested. The old darling, she looks like a doll saved from a fire."

Across the river, the lights of Brooklyn's modest skyline had begun to come on. "I thought once of living right here in this hotel," he said. "But it never occurred to me it's where you can see all of Brooklyn and all the middle of Manhattan at once."

"Capote territory, you mean?"

His eyes lingered on the water between. "Home is home, just a little worse than it ever was. Two days back, and it's as though I'd never left. I've got to find my own place."

In no time, he'd found it, decorated it, and phoned me to come have a look.

October 19 [reads my journal], John Cage on Fifth Avenue.

"Where are you going?" he says.

"To see Truman Capote. You?"

"Downtown . . . a rehearsal with Merce, the piano. You got time for a cup of tea?"

The table we occupy at Hicks's is no bigger than a plant stand. On it, John places a book.

"I've been reading about the Greeks," he says. "They're funny."

"How so?"

"Phaedra. Theseus. Phidias. You ever in your life heard *camp*ier names? Speaking of Greeks, what does a sober member of academe like you have in common with a Ganymede like Capote?"

Unexpected, the note of challenge and censure in the question causes me to sit back in my chair and fold my arms.

"I like him," I said.

Truman's name was lettered in gold on black. Admitted by a buzzer, I climbed to the second floor and walked into an "efficiency" of two rooms and a sort of playpen kitchen furnished in what appeared to be stuff hauled in from a theatrical warehouse: gilt chairs, painted shutters, mirrors scrolled with Venetian flourishes, velvet in draped swatches, harem pillows, a blackamoor holding a torch.

"It's all mine," he said, "picked by hand. I saw Garbo coming out of this junk shop on Third Avenue, so I went in. What are you doing for dinner?"

A quick meal at the Oyster Bar in Grand Central, I told him, because I had a ticket for *A Streetcar Named Desire*. "Come with *me*," he said, "I've got a dinner date with old Streetcar himself— you'll see his new character: pepper-and-salt tweeds, a brand-new voice. Can you imagine an Oxford *drawl*? . . . A long black cigarette holder to finish off the *tout ensemble*."

Unwilling to waste my ticket, I decided to forgo the playwright for the play.

Lightly made, this decision was one I'd come to regret. Already acquainted with Williams long enough to have seen for myself his transformation from a Bible salesman in blue serge to the natty parody of affluence that Truman ridiculed, I'd never been alone with the two of them, and would not again have the opportunity.

Over the years, Truman's view of Tennessee alternated with a whimsicality I could not fathom. His interest in the man and his work was continuous and lively, yet lacked altogether the affection that might have explained its constancy. A slightly detached air of amused tolerance toward Tennessee was the norm, but this would often change to a kind of vindictive outrage out of all proportion to its causes. The former seemed to come from Truman's assumption that his own sophistication and social grace were of an order beyond the reach of his friend. The latter showed itself in tongue-lashings evoked by some newly uncovered evidence of Tennessee's "tackiness" in dealings with people, some new report of his abrupt abandonment of a friend or lover. In any case, through good times and bad in the course of careers closely parallel, Tennessee was never out of Truman's purview, or beyond the reach of his contumely.

What in 1948 Truman took to be the arriviste pretensions of a man who'd made it, struck me as no more than the privileges anyone suddenly rich and famous might be moved to assert. This difference of opinion became a sore point in a long, intermittent argument, never resolved. For reasons that remained obscure and all his own, Truman made certain that the man most likely to be his natural ally would be kept at a distance.

Never a friend of Williams, I saw him often but at no time long enough to disabuse him of the notion that I was always au courant with Truman's progress and somehow in his confidence. For more than thirty-five years, Truman was our one subject—on a beach in Nantucket, in a London pub, at a sidewalk table on the Via Veneto and on a score of occasions in Manhattan when, as far as I knew, Truman was in retreat on Mount Athos, or touring Tasmania.

In spite of my repeated disclaimers, Tennessee held to this misapprehension for the rest of his life, during the last years of which each of our encounters took place in Key West. And it was there in 1975, on Tennessee's home territory, that Truman and he would come congenially together for all but the last time before their friendship suffered a mortal blow—struck by Truman.

In the assemblage of grotesques he puts on show in "Unspoiled Monsters," Truman in most cases provides touches of red herring meant to separate actual people from their caricatures, and perhaps to avoid charges of libel. But in the instance of "Mr. Wallace . . . the most acclaimed American playwright," his efforts at obfuscation are minimal. No one could believe that the "chunky, paunchy, booze-puffed runt with a play moustache glued above laconic lips" he portrays was other than Tennessee Williams. This gentleman lives at the Plaza in a squalor of his own making (enhanced by the incontinence of the bulldog he is too far gone into alcoholic stupor to walk) and sends out for both food and exotic sexual services. Hounded by demons, he sees himself as the object of a vendetta mounted by traitorous critics and believes he is marked for murder by anonymous enemies who maintain their cover without obscuring their menace. A hypochondriac, he's convinced he's dying of cancer, the source of which varies from day to day. Misery has made him eloquent, but not convincing—at least not to the alter ego Truman had devised, a hustler who has his own opinion: "Here's a dumpy little guy with a dramatic mind who, like one of his own adrift heroines, seeks attention and sympathy by serving up half-believed lies to total strangers . . . he has no friends because the only people he pities are his own characters and himself."

Before this appeared in print, a 1975 photograph of a smiling

Tennessee and a smiling Truman had hung in the restaurant of Key West's Pier House for nearly two years. One evening, not long after the publication of "Unspoiled Monsters," Tennessee and a party of friends went there for dinner. As they were being seated he told a waiter they did not propose to give their orders until the photograph was removed. Within minutes, the offensive object was retired.

But Truman out of sight, I learned, was not Truman out of mind. Williams continued to bring his name into every conversation, as a journal entry from 1981 makes clear.

> March 2.   My sunset party to celebrate the adjacent birthdays of Dick Wilbur and Jimmy Merrill.
>
> Tennessee arrives with his Canadian friend Verne Powers and a young man strumming a guitar, along with two companions they've found in a parking lot: a superannuated hippie in buskins and Indian beads, and a little black-and-white terrier with moony eyes and responsive ears.
>
> "If you've got a place to sit down," says Williams, "this older gentleman will be beholden."
>
> As his pickups find their way into things, I place him and the minstrel at a terrace table where John Ciardi is instructing an astonished woman on the etymological provenance of a word she's just had the misfortune to utter. Interrupting his disquisition for introductions, I'm about to move on when Tennessee catches my arm.
>
> "Truman," he says. "Is he trying to commit suicide in public?"
>
> "What now?"
>
> "They've hauled him off another stage, smashed out of his skull. This time in San Francisco. Has he talked to you about it?"
>
> Reluctant to report even so much as last week's missed-connection call from T., I shake my head.

"Your own bottle of red wine," I tell him, "I've been keeping it out of sight."

When I return with it, the guitarist is fingering strings and beginning to vamp toward song—a development, apparently sponsored by Tennessee, which quickly causes the company to realign itself.

Long after dark, the party finally shows signs of breaking up. Surrounded by a few who've lingered, the singer is perched on a coral rock. The little dog is curled up in the kitchen, as if for good. Tennessee, his bottle drained, nods heavily at whatever it is that has sent the rest of his table into an explosion of laughter. I take a seat at the adjoining table, where Verne has been keeping a watchful eye on the progress of things. Beside me, ninety-year-old Grace Stone tries to catch the drift of conversation between Martin Gottfried and Carl Bernstein, and soon gives up.

"Mr. Williams," she murmurs, "is he hard of hearing? —Or is it something else?"

"Probably something else."

"That's what I thought," she says, and casts an appraising glance at Tennessee, who's not where he was a second ago but on his feet and directly behind me, his hands encircling my neck.

"John Malcolm," he says. "I've had lovers . . . everyone knows I've *al*ways had lovers. But you know what? I've never had love."

I sense a touch of lips on the top of my head. "Now I don't even ex*pect* to. That's my trouble . . . and it's the same with poor old You-know-who."

Quick to the rescue, Verne gently pulls Tennessee's hands from my Adam's apple and sees him out. The little dog wiggles after them as far as the gate and then comes wiggling back. The guitarist sings on into the night.

Almost a year later (the journal reminds me) we met again.

January 3.   To David Wolkowsky's cocktails for Henry McIlhenny; the penthouse chiaroscuro with candle shadows and white blossoms.

Tennessee, alone on a couch, beckons me over.

"I'm in some bewilderment about Truman," he says. "We've been doing the dirty dozens on one another for thirty years, and now he's dedicated his new book to me. If *Music for Chameleons* is some sort of joke, I can't find the point of it. Can you?"

"Perhaps he's offering an olive branch." My sentence sags with lack of conviction. "Maybe it's his subtle way of eating crow."

"Aren't you in touch with him?"

"No."

"From what I've been hearing, he doesn't seem to know anyone these days, least of all himself."

*"Mis*ter Williams!"

(The intruder who makes room for herself beside us is a middle-aged resident of that well-mown and well-mannered part of Key West the inhabitants of Old Town call "Los Angeles.")

"I understand you're about to leave us," she says. "For parts unknown?"

"Bangkok," says Tennessee, "by way of London. There's a Concorde connection takes you straight through."

"Bangkok!" she says, as if the name itself were an affront. "What*ev*er for?"

Lifting his right hand, he rubs the thumb against the tips of his fingers. "I love the feel of silken bodies," he says.

My place in Key West was a sort of glassed-in box on a strip of sand next to the now defunct resort called The Sands. A waterside catwalk enclosing the property afforded a full view of its small adjacent beach.

Out for a breath of air one February evening, I noted one lone swimmer in the twilight chill, then the shorts and towel he'd left on a jut of coral. I watched as he found a footing in the shallows, advanced to pick up his gear, and, wrapping himself in a robe with a cowl, sat like a figure on a monument. Shivering in the sudden dark, I was about to leave him to his tableau when he called out my name.

"You're supposed to be in Bangkok!" I called back.

"I was diverted . . . to Houston," he said. "I mean: Chicago."

Climbing down from his perch, he approached the catwalk on which I was standing. "What's the latest word on T.C.?"

For once, I had that word. But to admit as much would be to render my repeated disclaimers ingenuous. Instead of rehearsing still another episode in the dwindling history of Truman's attempts to "get clean" and to come to living terms with John O'Shea, I held my tongue—only to learn that Tennessee had read my mind.

"That new Irish bruiser he's been on and off with . . . who *is* he? They came to the house together a few years ago . . . Humpty and Dumpty, it seemed to me. But the disparity soon became apparent. Who *is* he?"

"You mean—his name?"

"I know his name. What part of the forest does that stripe of cat come from?"

Reluctant to provide this information, I saw no reason to offer any other.

The little waves kept scattering themselves. Music from the piano bar had begun to drift over. With a slight shudder, Tennessee pulled his robe tighter about him.

"B-r-r-r-r," he said, and hugged himself. "I've left my duds in the care of a bartender. I'd better get into them. *Ciao.*"

"*Ciao.*"

Nine days later—according to Williams's biographer, Donald Spoto—Tennessee sat down with Truman for the last, and final, time during a "fashionable party" in New York. There Tennessee asked his old "friend and sometime nemesis" when, if ever, they might meet again. Truman's answer—two years before Tennessee's death and three before his own—was both amusing and exact.

"In Paradise."

In that same autumn of 1948, I had myself moved to new quarters, a house in Westport. From there, once a week, I'd go to New York to sit on the septuagenarian board of a publishing house which expected me to come up with ideas that might free it from almost exclusive fiscal dependence on the continuing popularity of *Black Beauty, Treasure Island,* and the plays of George Bernard Shaw. Since I soon found that the ideas I presented sank without ripples into the impenetrable lethargy of that boardroom only to resurface on the lists of other publishers, my place there was as redundant as my prospects were bleak. Depressed after one of these sessions, I called on Truman. Generous in his new affluence, he took me to lunch at The Colony.

As we were being escorted to our table, I caught sight of the playwright John Van Druten, waving in our direction rather like a baby saying bye-bye. Truman, pretending not to notice, made no return gesture.

In a minute Van Druten was at our table, bending in a courtly bow. "Truman, young man," he said. "I've missed the sight of you this long while."

"That . . . must . . . be," said Truman, underlining the banality of things, "because I've been *away!*"

"And where is away?"

"Paris."

"And how did you find Paris?"

"To tell the God's truth, cold and gloomy."

"And you're back now, for the winter?"

"I really can't say."

"I hope I'll have a chance to see more of you. Will you ring me? Actually, I've been lunching here almost every day."

"That's nice," said Truman, and lifted his frozen daiquiri.

"It's been good to see you, my boy." Holding his napkin, Van Druten went back to his table.

I watched until he was seated, then turned to Truman. "Rudeness is no prerogative," I said, "even for a kid celebrity."

"I've had quite enough of Mister V.D., thank you."

The space between us yawned.

Screening his face with a menu card, he said: "I suggest we change the subject. What are you going to have?"

The *coquilles St. Jacques* I ordered cooled. It was three o'clock before—in a gloom punctuated by gambits not taken up—we left the restaurant. Since the afternoon was summery and we had nothing in particular to do, we started for Central Park and strolled around the pond that catches the shadow of the Plaza.

"This is one of the places where I used to play hookey," he said. "Every day when it wasn't raining."

"*Every* day?"

"Well, every other day. I just could not sit in a schoolroom. Days I had to, I'd anesthetize myself, put myself in a coma, and dream up paperweight cities and towns where everything happened the way I wanted it to. Mostly, I just didn't go. . . . I'd go to the library, that private one, it's called the New York Society Library. That's where I met Willa Cather. Would you believe we became good friends? She used to be there with that girl friend of hers. . . . They're still

living together somewhere near me, on Park Avenue. No. I think she
died last year."

"Willa Cather did."

"Anyway, when it wasn't that, it was the Roxy or the Radio City
Music Hall, two stage shows and the movie. Remember Evelyn and
Her Magic Violin? Borrah Minevitch and His Harmonica Rascals?
Ted Lewis . . . is *everybody happy?*"

One day early in December, I answered my office phone. "I'm
holed up," said Truman, "can you come over?"

I told him I had to see a young novelist from Texas, then keep an
appointment to be photographed for *Look* magazine.

"What have you done now?"

"Cracked the Fenian code in *Finnegans Wake,*" I said. "How
about one-thirty?"

"Bring some eats. I've got something to tell you."

A few hours later I rang his bell.

"You're lucky to find me," he said.

"Why?"

"Marlon Brando."

"What's he got to do with anything?"

"Well, duckling, drag up a chair—but don't lean back, it's break-
able."

Handing me a drink, he lit a cigarette. "Mister Stanley Kowalski
came by yesterday in this *gear,*" he said, and made a sweep of his
hand, knees to forehead. "Before you can say Robinson Crusoe—"

"Jack Robinson."

"Before you can say Jack Robinson, I'm on the seat of this jukebox
Harley-Davidson zipping in and out of traffic down to the Battery,
me hanging on to that beer barrel like some pickup bobby-soxer.
Scared? Out of my chicken wits, a complete conviction I'd never see
the light of another day. I can't tell whether it was on purpose or not

—careening way over, zooming to dead stops, then just standing still and revving up or whatever they call it. There's something pretty cuckoo about that one, let me tell you. Anyway, I was limp, not to mention frozen in the extremities, when we got back here. Whereupon Mr. K. stretches out—there, on that couch. Without so much as an aye, no, kiss my foot, simply displays the length of him in all that leather drag, stares at the ceiling as if I didn't exist, goes to sleep . . . to *sleep,* mind you . . . for three solid hours."

"What did you do?"

"What *could* I do? I looked the situation over, tried to figure out what it meant, shrugged my shoulders, and sat down on that." He pointed to a golden rocking chair. "Sat there like Whistler's Mother and read Edith Wharton's *Custom of the Country.* Maybe they're all cuckoo. Monty Clift—another one not dealing from a full deck. Won't go outside the door, not even to eat. Sits all day in his underwear and tootles on a trumpet. Well, enough of nutsy actors. What you got in that bag?"

I spread out my smorgasbord. He brought plates and silver from the miniature kitchen. "That's not the thing I have to tell you," he said. "I'm giving a party, a big one."

"So what else is new?"

"Wait and I'll *tell* you." He got up to freshen his glass. "I've met someone."

"So?"

"So the way to make it happen again, without *imposing* myself, is to give a rather large party at the Park Avenue place, invite him and his spouse . . . yes, there's that to consider, eight years of it, and don't make a face . . . and anyway, I decided this would be the most graceful way to work it."

"Couldn't you think of something less elaborate?"

"Never you mind. If things proceed, *as* planned, let me assure you it will be worth *ev*ery effort."

It was late when, on the designated Sunday evening, I got to the party. In the elevator with me were a man in a trench coat and a woman in mink. She I recognized—Joan McCracken, the dancer known as "the little girl who falls down" in *Oklahoma!* He I did not. His hair was red, face craggy, eyes sea-green. A sullenness about him hinted at tension under control. He might have been thirty, fifty. No matter, I knew he was the excuse for the party.

The door to the Capote apartment was open. We left our coats with a maid and became part of a crowd spilling over into hallways and the kitchen, from which Truman emerged at once. "Know something? I didn't have to do this after all," he said. "Everything's settled. When there's a chance, I'll point him out."

That did not happen. Coming late, as I thought, I had come early. Or had I merely joined one evening's segment of some timeless gathering of the clan? Beatrice Lillie was there, Tallulah Bankhead expected. Bennett Cerf was telling funny stories to Libby Holman, Josh White lecturing Stella Adler. As Wystan Auden, his feet in carpet slippers, was about to depart without a coat, the marquis of Milford-Haven was checking his. The party had the air of a rehearsal call for a play that would never be performed. Following Auden's lead, I soon headed for the elevator and encountered him on the sidewalk. "I told Truman I'd come for half an hour," he said. "The point of occasions of this sort evades me, unless one knows everyone . . . then I still don't see."

A cab drew up and disgorged a young woman, a young man, and a man who looked like Johann Sebastian Bach. Auden climbed in and drove off.

"Speed!" said the young woman. "We promised to call mother at midnight."

"I'd rather do that from Lenny's," said Speed.

Followed at a petty pace by the man who looked like Bach, they disappeared into the lobby.

When the doorman's whistle produced another cab, I went home.

At a tea party on the following day, the host was Leo Lerman, the guest of honor Evelyn Waugh. The other guests were mostly writers delighted for a chance to meet the novelist whose work had provided many of them with models, and all of us with the fading but still useful phraseology of Trocadero chic. From the start, the afternoon was a fiasco approaching the sick-making. Ensconced in the center of the room, Mr. Waugh had no intention of engaging in conversation; he was there to give audience. Introduced to four or five people in succession, he waved each of them aside before they could open their mouths. In minutes there was a zone of interdiction about his chair no one dared to cross twice.

Smarting from my own abrupt dismissal, I found Truman at my side. "Did *you* get the treatment?" he asked. "That mushroomy paw dropping yours before you've had a chance to shake it? Little eyes fixed on the ceiling when you try to talk?"

We watched as, one by one, others were presented and summarily rebuffed. "Who does that little pig think he is?" said someone behind us. "He's supposed to be worried about the decline of manners."

A shuffling in the crowd, by then so big as to overwhelm the man in the middle, produced an opening. Through it came Jean Stafford. "They're setting up a relief bar," she announced in her Daisy Buchanan voice. "Major cases should line up at once."

"Major cases of what?" I asked.

"Outrage," she said.

Truman and I were among those who began to trade in their cups of Earl Grey for tumblers of Old Grand-dad. "The other night," he said, "were you able to pick him out?"

"Red hair?"

He nodded. "Come the first day you can," he said. "We'll talk."

I got to Truman's at noon and put cold cuts, French bread, Port Salut, and cherry pie on the coffee table; he put Fats Waller on the turntable.

"I've made up my mind," he said. "I mean, *we've* made up *our* minds. Ever think you'd hear me say that? We're pulling up stakes and heading for Europe."

"For the winter?"

"For good—let's say, 'indefinitely.' "

"Give up this apartment?"

He nodded. "Jack will keep his . . . just in case something might force us to come back."

"Ain't misbehavin'," sang Waller, *"I'm saving my love for you."*

"I'm taking that with me," said Truman, "Fats and Lee Wiley. Then Flaubert, Virginia Woolf, Chekhov . . . maybe some Faulkner. Do you think Faulkner might seem different overseas? When I'm reading him, I feel threatened by something in the back of my head that won't declare itself, something maybe too close to home. Listen, you ought to get to know Jack . . . black Philadelphia Irish with the temper to go with it. Why not now? He has no phone but I know he's there."

Our taxi dropped us in the middle of a block of tenements where trains of the Third Avenue elevated made thunderstorms overhead. In a schoolyard paved with concrete, some kids were playing stickball in the sooty remnants of a recent snowstorm. Jack's name was on the mailbox in an entryway shared by a Chinese laundry. The bell did not work. When we'd climbed three flights of a clammy stairwell that had tin walls painted apple green, like those in Victorian waiting rooms, Truman rapped on a scarred green door. Jack opened it.

He was my man in the elevator, all right, but without the sullen demeanor I remembered. He gave Truman a hug and shook my hand. Waiting to be shown into the flat, I realized all at once that we *were* in it: one room with a bunk bed, a sagging settee, a table and chairs in an ell that served as a kitchen. There was a gray stoneware sink, a brass spigot, a claw-footed bathtub across the top of which was a board covered with checkered oilcloth. Outside, on the dripping fire escape, were five red geraniums in a row. There was no bathroom, but a W.C. in the hall, which—as I learned in a few minutes—had no window and was unheated. To flush the toilet, you had to reach for a wooden handle and pull the chain. Yet the flat itself had a miniature coziness about it entirely inviting—hand-painted flourishes of leaves, abstract stars on the bunk and chairs, a shipshape Scandinavian cleanliness.

When Jack produced drinks, we sat around the table as though we were about to play cards. "I've told Malcolm about our idea of Europe. . . . I didn't tell him you thought Ischia," said Truman, and turned to me. "What do you know about Ischia?"

"It's in the Mezzogiorno. It's volcanic. It's mentioned in Gibbon."

"What *I* want," said Truman, "is a place with sun. Period. Then something pretty to look at when I raise my heavy head from the typewriter. People . . . I couldn't care less. People I can do with-out."

Over the rim of his whiskey glass, Jack's eyes met mine.

"I want quiet," continued Truman, "beautiful quiet and a nice little post office with outsize postage stamps and a donkey with a straw hat and flowers in his ears I can ride into the village and . . ."

Truman was in good hands, I thought. Once more he'd found the right person at the right time. Mary Lou Aswell had already spoken for all of us. "Don't be deceived by that look of helplessness," she had told a reporter. "Little T. has an uncanny way of choosing just those people who understand him, and will help him. It's in his stars, or his destiny, or his health line, or whatever you want to call it, that he travel in the right direction . . . his instinct leads him to the people who are on his side."

Alone, she might have added, he travels alone, except that there's always someone with him.

As Truman became absorbed in his new life, I turned my attention to a long-contemplated project now supported by a publisher's advance—a critical biography of Gertrude Stein. Editorial conferences still brought me to New York every Wednesday, when we'd meet for jazz and gossip, but it was not until he and Jack were about to sail away that I realized I was concerned about him in ways I'd not yet had a chance to express. On February 21, 1949, my journal reports:

A farewell visit. In the course of it I tell Truman I've begun to follow him in the columns of the tabloids the way other people follow comic strips.

"Well . . ." he says. "I ain't no Li'l Abner . . . but I sure get around Dogpatch."

"Other people get around, nobody knows about it. How come it's always you?"

He smiles a pussycat smile.

"Half the stories are planted, I'm told. Twenty-five dollars an item. Is that true?"

"Of course it's true. If I can spread a little of the national wealth around, why not? Twenty-five dollars is a lot of money to pick up for just a phone call."

"But won't there come a day when that item called Truman Capote will turn into a public commodity? Won't the figure begin to take on a life of its own—separate from the person?"

"So what? *I* know who I am."

"That's what Gertrude Stein thought. Then when she became famous, she wasn't so sure. 'I am I because my little dog knows me,' she told herself, but it didn't do. 'That doesn't prove anything about me,' she said, 'it only proves something about the dog.' Truman, you don't even have a dog."

"When I get one, I'll ask him. Will that make you feel better? What you have to understand is, I don't so much want a reputation as I want a career. If a reputation can help me get it, what's wrong with a reputation? Have you got your car here?"

I did.

"Would you drop me at Jack's? We can say bon voyage on the way."

We drive through slush, park in front of the Chinese laundry, which, as usual, is closed. "What you were saying about Gertrude Stein . . ." says Truman. "Who except pedants ever knew about her until she made herself famous? It wasn't the work that did it. . . . Can you honestly say you know anyone who's read *Tender Buttons* through? The thing that made her famous was the *story* of the work and all that went *with* it. It may be a sad commentary, one you academics have trouble accepting, but people are people."

Rain beats hard on the roof of the car. The noise of an elevated train comes on like a cyclone, leaves a widening stillness. "This is it," he says. "Don't fret about me, just don't for*get* me."

Before he's reached the tenement door, I call out.

"Truman!"

He turns.

"Get a dog!"

His return from Europe in December, as it turned out, would be made under my auspices and at my expense. Meanwhile, with no word from him for months, I wrote in the hope of learning that his choice of Ischia had proved to be happy.

"Yes, yes," he wrote back, "I'm not only happy but in a condition in which I have rarely found myself—a state of contentment. It's an enchanting island, Ischia, and we've had the great luck to find a whole floor to ourselves in a *pensione* that looks far down to the edge of the sea. You would love it, and I cannot understand why you do not pack up at once and *descend.* We plan to stay at least until midsummer. We both read a great deal and I'm glad to report that I'm working rather a tremendous lot. The swimming is superb: water clear as kittens' eyes, and great volcanic rocks that serve as diving boards.

"Bands of amusing people come drifting in and out, but it's serene, *very* serene, for the most of it. Jack is splendid: a face like saddle leather and, among other things I've discovered, he can handle a boat. This past weekend we sailed clear around the island."

This letter was followed the next day by another.

"This ain't, in your case, *déjà vu,*" wrote Truman, "but a postscript to say and ask what I didn't yesterday.

"Yes, Wystan, he is very much here. I know you admire him and sometimes I do, too—on the *page.* But in person and day to day he's not the easiest pill to swallow: He ought to be running a school, perhaps a military academy—all these meticulous rules about what to do and precisely how to do it. Truth to tell, I'm weary of him and have watched him closely enough to say flatly: he's a dictatorial bastard.

"If I sound cranky, it's only in this instance. The days are beautiful—full summer before summer has even begun—except that now and then there are a rough two or three days with foam over the rocks and the natives sitting like crows. It's the sirocco, and when it comes there's really nothing else to do but take it, which in all these centuries they have *not* learned to do.

"I, on the other hand, keep my nose to the grindstone mornings, then turn to other occupations, *comme ça:* Princess Margaret is coming to the island today and everyone keeps calling up at me because I've been lining up baskets of nosegays and marguerites to toss from the balcony. *Quel camp.* Also, I'm in the most critical stage of baking a devil's food cake, and that demands my unswerving attention. Therefore you must excuse the brevity of this note. Write to me. Mail time is my day's excitement.

"P.S. Have you heard anything about my book? It is so very strange—nobody mentions it, not even, in his letter to me, my editor. I have a feeling that it has evaporated or, indeed, was never printed at all. Do you know anything about this boy William Goyen? His story in the March *Horizon,* while a very bad story indeed, is certainly well written."

Fully engaged on my biography of Gertrude Stein, I accepted another invitation to Yaddo, where, on June 15, I made this entry in my journal:

> Arrived here late morning, I learn I've been given Truman's old tower room. When I climb the dark stairs, the harp on the back of the door merely whines. Someone has removed the leaden balls.
>
> I take my typewriter out of its case, place it on the ivory-white desk. A whoosh of wind comes soughing through the surrounding pines; a mourning dove whimpers outside the door to the terrace; a shaft of light hits the choir stall. Framed in the huge main window, green hills roll toward the old battlefields. A scratching, apparently made with a diamond ring across the bottom of the pane, makes a declaration of love dated August 22, 1897. Sitting in the crazy bishop's chair, I listen to other voices in other rooms.

Truman and Jack were now in North Africa, a fact of which I was not aware until I got a letter late in June. "A curious place," wrote Truman, "there's every kind of activity, most of it raffish, to say the very least, and all manner of humankind—outré, or decadent, elegant or abandoned to hashish or sex, or both of these at once. A little on the scary side, too, and you have to get accustomed to noises the likes of which you've never heard, faces of a character you've never seen, *or* imagined—and hashish fumes and the smell of *thé arabe.* For all that, there's a charm that gets to you.

"Janie and Paul Bowles live in this hotel, which means we have company, even too much of it. Gore Vidal has been here—*has,* I'm overjoyed to say, and is not likely to return. When I think *I'm* paranoid, I listen to him and feel better at once. Did I have a chance to tell you what happened just before we left New York? Hold your hat.

"It's Sunday morning, me nicely *déshabillé* over coffee. The doorbell rings. Who pushes in, hopped-up and crazy-eyed, but G.V. 'Truman,' he says, 'they're out to get us!' and starts off on this totally incomprehensible routine about 'them' and how we have to 'stand pat' and 'close ranks,' etc. 'What in the hell are you talking about,' says I, 'I think you've come to the wrong door. If you don't mind, I'd like to close it.' Can you imagine?

"Cecil Beaton is here, staying in a house owned by the Guinnesses. Wouldn't you know that we two iron-winged butterflies would find ourselves in the same hollyhock? If not for him, I'd move on, although I *do* like these sugar-soft beaches, toward one of which I'm about to repair, to the accompaniment of flutes."

I had by this time accepted an invitation by the governing board of New York's Young Men's and Young Women's Hebrew Association to become director of activities in that part of their educational program known as the Poetry Center. In the course of putting together a season of programs that would include readings by such figures as Dylan Thomas, Robert Frost, e. e. cummings, Stephen Spender, Allen Tate, and Mark Van Doren, it occurred to me that

Truman, who, as far as I knew, had never made a public appearance as a writer, might allow me to add his name to our already illlustrious roster.

He was at once receptive, except as to the matter of the fee I'd been empowered to offer him. I had to make a plea to the financial overseers of the Poetry Center for a higher amount that would also include the cost of transatlantic passage. When this was granted, Truman and I agreed on the date of December 8.

"Paris is dark, cold and, oddly, silent," he wrote, "and progress on my book has been maddeningly slow. Maybe I'm just tired of sparking up the foreign scene. Now I'm dealing with a bad case of grippe, but do not think it will interfere with plans to get to the Poetry Center on the 8th. In any case, I am about to alleviate my symptoms by having Thanksgiving dinner at Maxim's.

"Air France (Air Chance, they call it here) should put me into Idlewild on the morning of the 5th, about eleven. Will I see you there? Second thought: It's an arduous trip through the jungles of Queens, so I will honestly not expect you.

"To prove I've taken your advice, I'll have with me a dog—a Pekingese puppy with a story: he was given to Janie Bowles by a friend of Cecil's and then when J. couldn't take him to England— the dog, that is—because of the British quarantine, she gave him to me. His name is Muffin and he looks like one—incredibly clever and funny.

"Delighted to hear you have your own *pied-à-terre*. Just 'off' Sutton Place? How *far* off?"

On the bright windy morning of December 5, I watched from the observation deck at Idlewild as the Constellation bearing Truman, Paris via Gander, touched down and taxied up. When the ramp was settled into place and the door wrenched open, out he stepped, bareheaded, with a little dog squashed in his left arm. When I waved, he picked me out and waved back, then lifted the dog's paw and waved it in my direction before he disappeared into the customs shed.

Half an hour later we were en route to Manhattan, but not as the crow flies. "I can't face up to going home," said Truman, "not yet, anyway. Let's have lunch."

Turning off the parkway, I headed for the Forest Hills Inn. There, Muffin ignored the hamburger prepared for him and sat patiently as we ordered martinis.

"I made a vow I wouldn't come back before *Summer Crossing* was finished," said Truman. "Here I am. The trouble was Paris, it's absolute hell taking care of two dogs and two parrots and trying to do anything else."

"Parrots?"

"We brought them from Morocco. All that in one hotel room, a menagerie." Muffin looked up and licked his tongue. "Absolute hell. . . ."

I inquired about Jack.

"He'll be coming over on the *Queen Mary*," he said, "next Thursday from Cherbourg . . . with the other dog, and twenty-four pieces of luggage . . . all our worldly possessions."

"You think you're ready? . . . to come home?"

He surveyed the restaurant, as though he might find the answer there.

"I'm not sure," he said. "I have to find out."

Late that afternoon I delivered him to Park Avenue, and two nights later met him at a party, where he introduced me to his old friend Phoebe Pierce. Perhaps twenty-two or -three, she had water-blue eyes, skin like a peace rose, and wore earrings with little diamonds that swung as she spoke. "I wish they were mine," she said, "but they're only borrowed, for the occasion."

"Phoebe's a thief," said Truman. "She was arrested for grand larceny when she was fifteen years old."

As Truman had long ago told me, she was not otherwise arrested:

Their high school love affair was the beginning of a friendship that had remained warm.

"Truman, I must run," she said as the clock struck midnight. "I've got a date with this dreamboat cadet from Brazil who's staying at the Plaza with his old lady. His name is Manuelo, I'm going to bring him to your reading."

Moments later, waving from the doorway in a mink coat far too big for her, she blew Truman a kiss.

"That's borrowed, too," said Truman. "Look I don't want to go home tonight. Would it be all right if I stayed with you?"

"What's the matter?"

"I don't know," he said. "Sometimes, even when everything's all right, I get frightened."

When I got up next morning, I found a note on the kitchen table: "I'll need *escort*. Call for me at seven."

When I did, he was in bed, "too sick to move."

"*Sick* sick?" I asked. "Or anxiety sick?"

"Both."

He stared at the ceiling as though he were in a trance, then shut his eyes.

"Should we call it off?"

"Give me a brandy," he said, "to stave off the shakes."

Maneuvering himself to the edge of the bed, he accepted the slug I poured and downed it in one gulp. "Look in that closet, you'll find my suit, black velvet with a dull gold lining."

Our taxi pulled up alongside one of the sawhorse barriers holding back the crowd that overflowed the lobby and spilled onto Lexington Avenue. Poetry Center ushers had to help us get by the flashing bulbs of photographers and the monitoring eyes of a special detail of policemen. Ignoring the Green Room's many mirrors, Truman began a restless tour of the premises.

His trepidation was contagious. While I could see that his young admirers, many of them with haircuts that imitated his, were out in force, I couldn't help wondering: How would the sober Poetry Center audience receive this childlike packet of a man with his Fauntleroy velvet, his dancing pumps, his baby seal's voice, his tendency to illustrate his points with little arabesques of emphasis?

At zero hour I took the stage alone and began an introduction, which I heard myself making as though I were listening to a recording in another room. When, at last, the record and the echo in my own echo chamber stopped, Truman walked on, climbed a high stool in the glow of pink spotlights, adjusted his big horn-rimmed glasses (titters from the back rows), lifted a copy of *Tree of Night,* and began.

Backstage, as the sound engineer kept fiddling with his dials to make sure that the extraordinary voice would come out as low and loud as possible, the hands of the wall clock shifted audibly. Otherwise, it was just Truman's words and profound silence. Turning a page, he looked straight into the semidarkness, from which, like the report of cracking ice, came an involuntary shout of laughter, quickly stifled. This was followed by a ripple of applause, then by a roar like an explosion. Everyone was laughing, everyone was "breaking up," including Truman himself. Shifting on his perch, he spoke an aside, adjusted his glasses, and had to wait for wave on wave of renewed laughter to subside.

Whatever turn it was he had taken, it led to a wide-open road that ended in a blast of applause, cries of "Bravo!" "Encore!" Bowing low, blowing kisses with both hands, he returned again and again and, with a hop and a skip, left for good only when the stage manager had started the house lights blinking.

Later that week, I called at his apartment en route to an appointment he'd made for us to view the results of his picture-taking session—"everything from jaybird naked to Little Boy Blue"—with the photographer Harold Halma.

"First, we're going to make a trip downtown," he said, "a little mission of mercy."

"Who are we going to be merciful *to?*"

"Billie. She's in the slammer. I've been sending notes to keep her spirits up. Now she says she wants to see me, just *see* me . . . on the sidewalk in front of that men's shop on Sixth Avenue."

In the bright cold, we waited for the doorman to whistle up a cab. "I've also sent her a box of Rose Marie chocolates, the kind they deliver by horse and carriage."

Secretly touched to be part of this excursion, I had Billie Holiday memories of my own—the New Year's Eve when we met like waifs in a crowd; the between-shows chats with her at 52nd Street's Famous Door and, later, brief meetings at the Village Vanguard where, minus her gardenia, she'd arrive turbaned like the Queen of Sheba in a pelisse of paisley, with a jockey-size man in a big hat at her side.

"You ought to meet her sometime," said Truman. "She has a kind of weird intelligence, as if she'd never before had any place to put it."

Out of the taxi on Eighth Street, we walked a few steps up Sixth and peered at the high windows of the Women's Prison as Truman waved a white handkerchief . . . a sight that attracted responses from a number of figures at once. Was Lady Day indeed one of those crowding the barred windows?

"There she is!" called Truman, and made slow bannerlike circles in the air.

Truman stayed in Manhattan just long enough to know that he was *not* ready to come home. Meeting at parties by accident, we would meet for dinners by design, usually at the Algonquin. There one evening early in February he spoke of plans for returning to Europe, once again to stay "indefinitely." But no departure date had been set, and there were more immediate things on his mind. "I'm giving a *rather* special little dinner party tomorrow," he said. "You're not invited."

"I may break into tears," I said. "Who's coming?"

"Charlie and Oona, Garbo and Cecil, ZaSu Pitts and Phoebe."

"Where are you giving it?"

"*Chez* Jack."

"What are you all going to sit on?"

"Don't," he said, "be bourgeois."

While our old rapport appeared to be constant, our paths had sharply diverged: his toward doors that now opened to him everywhere, mine toward attendance upon Dylan Thomas, who, having come to America at my invitation, had at once involved me in a friendship that had about it, as an observer would one day astutely point out, "the character of an hallucination." Out of touch with Truman for many months, I caught up with him only in time to say bon voyage on the night before he and Jack were to board a freighter for Italy. This occasion, hurried and crowded, was less than satisfactory for me and, as I learned by a letter early in May, for him as well.

"You were more than dear to come that very last night," he wrote from Taormina, "and I have had twinges of remorse about the way things turned out, because I would have liked to have seen you alone.

"The crossing was extraordinary: twenty-one days, and our shipmates were an odd lot of gloomy Turks who began all of their remarks with 'We Turks' (think this or that): Consequently, I'm rather happily relieved to be here on the high solid earth of Taormina; it is beyond saying beautiful, a springtime I can only describe as unearthly. You would adore it; and we've come into possession of the most charming villa* just a twenty-minute stroll from the center. There's a wildly tangled garden, two bedrooms, two terraces, an enormous salon, kitchen, bathroom, and a hawk's-eye

---

* Fontana Vecchia, where D. H. Lawrence lived in the early twenties.

view of the blue mountains of the Italian peninsula, snow, sea. Fifty dollars a month. Can you believe it?

"André Gide has a place not far from here. Such a lonely figure in his velvet pants, Shakespearian cape, and maestro's fedora. He haunts the barbershop having his face lathered by boys of ten and twelve; and there's a scandal abroad in the piazza, not because he arranges to take these boys home with him, but because he seldom sends them back with more than two hundred lire (20¢). Otherwise, the whole place is blessedly free of literary folk or, come to think of it, folk of any kind. You must come and stay. Meanwhile, write me, because we Turks miss you."

Preoccupied with Dylan Thomas, trying to keep his affairs straight, those on his lecture circuit and those in particular hotel rooms and boudoirs of Manhattan and Brooklyn, I had little time for personal correspondence, as Truman was quick to remind me. "Why don't I hear from you?" he wrote. "The one and only reason I send letters is to make sure I *get* letters. Please understand that I want this on a paying basis.

"Cecil has been here and gone—a sojourn not memorable for him, I suspect, because he doesn't care for the beach and when we don't go there the only diversions are shopping in the market or sitting down to aperitifs and people-watching in the piazza. Worse than that, since we are stay-at-homes who can't cook much more than a three-minute egg, we depend upon a girl we've invited for the august office of mistress of the *cucina.* But we've discovered that she can't cook, either (although I must say her attempts to cover up the fact are ingenious, and now and then edible), and since we can't bear to fire anyone so spirited—and with so profound a belief in the powers of *malocchio*—we're back where we started.

"Anyway, I think Taormina would suit you every bit as much as it does me: Etna with its cone of snow in the hard-blue distance, a room with a view down to the sea, and across a hazy or sometimes glittering stretch of water to Calabria; a shop where you can buy English newspapers; even a bar where they know how to make an American martini. So, pack up your Olivetti—along with a few cans of Danish ham and Armour's corned beef (Italian meat is abominable) and come as soon as you can."

"Soon" would be no earlier than September, I wrote him from Cape Ann, and went on with a summer in recuperation from my first experience of Dylan Thomas and in preparation for my biography of Gertrude Stein.

"Why don't you meet us in Venice," he wrote on July 26, "then come back here for a few days? You would love our house. Am delighted to hear *The Sorrows of Cold Stone* is coming out this winter. Are you alone on Cape Ann? What *is* Cape Ann? I miss you."

When I could come, he was in Venice, toward which I made my way after a visit with Dylan and his latest American girl (a close friend of Truman's) in London and another to Paris for a series of talks with Alice B. Toklas.

As my journal reminds me, this stopover also entailed an odd and somewhat discomforting interview:

> September 9.   A note at the desk sends me to the nearby Bureau de Poste for a *pneumatique* from Alice T. . . . naming three different times when I might come, and answering a question I'd asked: "Yes the rue de Fleurus has changed. We thought 27 had a few months after we left it, immediately before they altered the pavilion. In that short time it had ceased to resemble the memory of the home we had lived in for so many years, which made us more than ever pleased to have been forced to leave it and live here."
>
> Later, when I reach her by phone, she says: "Sunday

would be particularly convenient. I'll expect you at four and a half. We'll be alone."

Early evening I go to the Hotel Pont Royal for drinks with Cyril Connolly and a tense young woman whom I take to be his wife. We are settling ourselves into the big leather chairs of the basement bar when, without prelude, Connolly glares at me, as though I'd said something insulting. "Truman Capote. What are you Americans going to do about him?"

"Do?"

"It appears to me that you are going to kill him with kindness, the insidious kindness that masks contumely, the kindness that turns all of your best writers into performing seals and drunken derelicts."

"I don't follow. . . . *Why* are we going to kill him?"

"I'll tell you why. Because you despise him, because you aren't prepared to cope with that completely alien kind of perception into an even darker underside of your character than Henry James could face up to. It fits no category you tolerate, conforms to no image of yourselves you can accept. It throws a whole new light on those interminable books about completely vapid and thoroughly nasty young men and the war."

He puts down the cigar he is about to light.

"What are their names?" He turns to his wife. "Eternity! *From Here to Eternity,* no less, and the other one—"

"The Naked and the Dead."

"Capote makes you uncomfortable and because you can't bear to be uncomfortable he is not to be forgiven. In the end, you'll destroy him. Mark my words."

His vehemence is so unexpected, his argument so emotionally charged, that I see no point in defending my murderous countrymen or in trying to tell him that, in his own sweet way, thank you, Truman will take care of Truman.

Our talk becomes rambling and without focus—not because we have little to say but because he and his wife are clearly in thrall to some running argument I have interrupted. To ease matters, I recall for her our meeting years ago when she gave a party in New York for the group of fresh from Harvard literati who came to Manhattan when I did.

She gives me a blank glance and turns to Connolly. "That would have been Jean," she says. "Cyril? Wouldn't that have been Jean?"

"Sonia here," he says, "is not Mrs. Connolly. Sonia is the widow of George Orwell."

When I arrived in Venice late next afternoon, the clerk at the Hotel Manin Pilsen handed me a note: *"Ciao!* Have *secured* a room —such as it may turn out to be. Am living across the Canal. Wld have been at the *stazione* to meet you except that Nina was departing at the same moment, from the airport. Will be down to get you (in a taxi, honey) at 6:30. T."

Off San Marco, overlooking a basin where inactive gondolas were lined up four and five abreast, the hotel was antiseptically clean, Teutonic, and graceless. My room was dark until I opened shutters onto a sound-box air shaft over a laundry where women were singing several melodies at once.

A brisk knock at the door. Truman bounced in. "Well, old buddy, welcome to Venezia," he said. "Have you ever seen anything more hopelessly beautiful? Wait, just wait. It's the most enchanting thing on earth, and maybe the saddest. You are going to lose your Chinese mind." He gave his growly laugh, stretched out flat on one of the beds. "Nina exhausts me," he said. "Are all mothers exhausting? Emotionally?"

Soon joined by Jack, we wove through shuffling crowds in byways to Harry's Bar, only to find ourselves stymied in its miniature muddle with no place to stand or sit. But not for long. At a word from Truman, a waiter lifted a table over the heads of other diners and set it up in a matter of seconds. "They know me here," said Truman. "Isn't that nice?"

A tall man with an Ur-British bearing swiveled around from his place at the bar and, nodding toward Truman, lifted his glass. Truman did the same. "You know who that is?" he said. "*No*body knows who that is. It's Henry Green."

Dinner over, we stopped in the piazza for an espresso at Florian's, strolled to the piazzetta, and stepped into a gondola that took us across the mouth of the Grand Canal to the Giudecca. The plash of its oars was so soft we might have been riding Charon's ferry.

The flat they'd rented was situated on a long waterside promenade. Its rooms were big, bedight with Italianate stuff, shiny fabrics and fringes as kitschy and comfortable as Mamma Leone's parlor. They had a new dog, a Kerry blue named Kelly, which had a habit of streaking about the place as though possessed.

"What's the latest word on our Sarah and Dylan Thomas?" asked Truman. "Did her dash to London turn out the way she'd planned it?"

Perhaps, I told him.

"What does *that* mean?"

"Dylan says he's in love with her. In the next breath he says he's in love with his wife, and always has been."

The lighted upper deck of a freighter headed for the marina slid by the windows.

"I think I met him once," said Truman, "in a sort of arty-shabby club in London. Mousy hair and yellow teeth? All I can say is, I wish her well. Did you see my little Alice B. Toklas in Paris? Did you meet any of those classy dikes around Natalie What's-her-name Barney? In the temple of love or whatever she calls it?"

(As he speaks I'm attuned to the other voice I've been hearing for days—Alice's, on the occasion of our first meeting: "There was a

72

young man here not long ago who claimed to know you. Does he? His name is Truman Capote."

I was on my way to Venice to see him, I told her.

"Now, *there's* a quaint one," she said. "A bit presuming, a little off-putting, at first—that voice and those curious little airs. I don't mean airs in the snob sense. I mean in the way he can't help conducting himself. But it strikes me there's a head on those shoulders. Would you say so?"

I would.

"So much about him reminded me of Gertrude Stein's young men —the pose of languor, the mix of wit and silliness somber people find so confusing or threatening. Dear George Antheil . . . He affected a similar haircut when he was your friend's age. . . . You know the Man Ray portrait? The same smooth open face you'd find on some *affiche* for baby powder, the same big doll's eyes. And to think what became of him—*Les Six* to Miss Lonelyhearts!")

"Alice likes you," I reported to Truman. "She thinks you're smart, that you've got a head on your shoulders."

"She's really a dear," he says, "if only she'd shave off that Fu Manchu moustache."

It was midnight when he and Jack walked me to the Zitelle vaporetto stop, where Kelly, darting between us, went skidding off the seawall and landed upright in a passing gondola. Shrieks, rumblings, sounds of scraping. As the gondolier picked up the dog and handed him over by the scruff, Jack attempted to apologize, to no avail. Along with a group of Venetians, we stood waiting for the vaporetto. The gondola came by once again.

"Cretino!" yelled the gondolier. *"Il cane stupido si butto in acqua,"* called out one of his passengers. *"Americani imbecilli!"*

> The long evening is over [reads a journal entry for September 22, 1950], the violins of San Marco silent. A big moon rides over the campanile, lighting the stacked

tables and chairs at Florian's, sending de Chirico shadows down the length of the colonnade. Snatches of song from the narrow *passaggetti* and bridges leading from the piazza tell that the candle-lit nightclubs have put up their shutters.

We dawdle toward the gondola landing beneath the pillar of Saint Theodore and his crocodile and are about to say good night when Kelly goes racing toward the Bridge of Sighs, stands barking on the white steps, comes tearing back in a sort of moon-crazy frolic. Jack tries to coax him into his leash. "Let him run," says Truman. "I've just decided: I don't want to cross that water once more today. Malcolm's going to put us up."

The night clerk is not at his desk. With Kelly on short tether, we go up by the stairs and settle in.

Moonlight, a sense of absurdity, the mosaic dazzle of Venice . . . something keeps me awake and adrift. Oppressed by lack of focus, loss of scale, unable to take in or account for what I've seen, I can but envy Truman's gift for instant appropriation. Other people come to see Venice. He all but suggests that Venice has been waiting to see him, and makes the notion seem natural. For the first time since I've known him he's without complaint and in the clear. His new novel is taking final shape; a book of his occasional writings is just off the press; another whole year in Italy is, he says, "a prospect of bliss." He seems to float in an aura of affection given and received. Instead of acting on compulsions to flaunt himself, he simply *is* himself. Yet, and yet . . . the distinction between his exhibitionism and his self-expression is thin. To "maintain reserve" would be as alien to Truman as a call to emulate the spiritual disciplines of Plotinus. If he feels like dancing to a rumba beat all by himself across the pavements of San Marco, he does—rewarded by applause from the tables at Quadri and cries of "Bravo!" from the loungers under the flagpoles. If he feels like tying a Hermès scarf to his belt loop or a Bulgari bangle to his wrist, no whisper of decorum deters him. He works as much as he plays. Hours at the typewriter are matched by hours at the cabanas of the Excelsior and long lunchtimes at Harry's, kissing people he knows and being kissed by people he doesn't know. His ambitions are as closely calculated as his pleasures are careless. And if he isn't ready to go home by midnight, he doesn't go home. . . .

6:00 A.M. [reads my next day's journal entry]. Laughter from the laundry below, a pounding on the door, send Kelly into a frenzy of watchdog importance. I can't make out what's being said in the hall, but it's rude, angry, and embellished with touches of *Serenissima* vulgate. Truman, attempting to muffle the dog, shouts back in kitchen Italian. The door remains bolted; we go back to sleep.

By nine, shaved and showered, we're ready to face the desk. When Truman produces a few thousand lire, ostensibly to pay for a copy of yesterday's *Il Gazzetino,* the air is cleared. We're dismissed with a long smile and a low bow.

When they cross to the Guidecca, I take the manuscript Jack has left with me and read it over an espresso at one of the tables outside Florian's. *Friends and Vague Lovers,* he calls it—well done, but perhaps too civilized for the grit it means to convey. Still, the grace and easy professionalism of it all is a surprise. When we meet at Harry's Bar for lunch, I'm about to tell him so when all the tables around us begin leaping into the air like tables at a séance. Kelly, having encountered two sleeping dogs, has not let them lie. Plates smash, wineglasses spill, silverware slides. Everyone stands up as the invisible dogfight goes on below. By the time calm is restored, I've forgotten what I meant to say.

We separate for the afternoon and, joined by Truman, meet again at All' Angelo, where our dinner companions are novelist Donald Windham, Tennessee Williams's close friend, a winsomely handsome young man with an air of unemployed intelligence; and the painter Henry Varnum Poor and his wife, the novelist Bessie Breuer, who, without prologue, tells us she has been "taking care of dear Ingrid ever since she broke up with Roberto." This piece of information provides no lead anyone follows and we are soon off to La Fenice and the American Ballet Theatre's version of *Romeo and Juliet*.

Midnight. Our gondola nuzzles up to the mossy steps of the Palazzo Venier dei Leoni. Peggy Guggenheim is waiting in the front garden next to "The Angel of the Citadel," her Marino Marini bronze of a youth astride a little horse. (The boy's removable and well-polished erection, as on all "occasions," is firmly in place.) Since she has never met more than two or three of her guests, including Truman, Miss Guggenheim greets us with as much curiosity as warmth and waves us on to join others already milling about white rooms hung with Kandinskys and Kokoschkas, Mondrians and Max Ernsts.

This occasion seems, at first, not so much a party as a midnight pilgrimage to hallowed premises—especially since our hostess keeps turning up in this room or that, surveying mute little groups with a worried smile, as though their presence were something for which she cannot entirely account. When supper is laid out on a long buffet, things begin to come together as, plates in hand, everyone retires to the library where the paintings are less tyrannizing and there are places to perch, shelves to put things on. Once the dancers have reduced the buffet to crumbs, there's a lull in which the distant pizzicati of Vivaldi on the record player make the stillness only more oppressive.

"Malcolm!" The voice is Truman's, from across the room, where, on a white leather couch, he seems to be sitting in Miss Guggenheim's lap. "Pick out something to dance to!"

Taking charge, he calls on John Kriza to help Miss G. clear the room. Joining her and her crew, I push and shove until there's an adequate space of marble floor, then flip through her record collection, Palestrina to Duke Ellington, and select "Take the 'A' Train." The dancers begin to jitterbug; the palazzo becomes a high school gymnasium on prom night. In a sedate two-step Truman and Miss Guggenheim weave in and out.

As our gondola back to San Marco slides by the frosted domes of the Salute, she remains on the steps of the landing to wave us out of sight.

"Poor dear," says Truman. "She's frightened of almost everything. I rather liked her. Didn't you?"

As time would show, Miss Guggenheim "rather liked" Truman, too. When Venice became the one city on the Continent above all others to which he'd return—"for the best martinis in Europe" at Harry's Bar, he said, and assurance that his presence there was as conspicuously favored as that of the Baronessa Franchetti or the Duchess of Manchest r—he and Peggy became fast friends and he was often her house guest.

My acquaintance with Miss Guggenheim would not be renewed for nearly three decades—when devotion to the city led me to make my summer home there on the same *piano seconda* of the Palazzo Barbaro in which she had herself lived when first she came to Venice to find a residence big enough to house her collection. Truman had meanwhile oddly "used" her in a part of his memoirs-by-surrogate in which he fantasizes that, in spite of their vast difference in age, he might have become her husband. This unlikely development, he suggests, would not have come about in pursuit of "all that Guggenheim glue," but "because she was good-hearted and because she tickled me—despite her habit of rattling her false teeth and even though she did rather look like a long-haired Bert Lahr." (The fact that her teeth were not false was immaterial.)

One evening in 1979 I called at the Palazzo Venier dei Leoni (then still as much a home as it was a museum) to take her to dinner. As we waited for the Chris-Craft water taxi to pick us up on the same green-with-moss marble ledge where she'd said good night to Truman and me twenty-nine years earlier, I recounted that occasion.

"Sounds like something from my twenties days," she said, "when we were always dancing the new thing and everyone seemed to live everywhere. Truman was *there* that night, you say? You're *sure*? He never told me."

Opaque to my efforts to bring the scene alive, she listened politely, but with the air of someone pretending to give thought to a proposal already rejected. Or so it seemed.

The table I'd booked at Harry's was, as she fully expected, the same one in the same corner which had been designated as hers in perpetuity since the first time she'd disembarked there from a gondola rowed by her own gondolier in his white livery and aquamarine sash. And, as I knew she would, she ignored the printed menu and ordered the pretty red shaving of uncooked beef called *Carpaccio*. Halfway through a plate of it, she put down her fork.

"That night! I was wearing my white Patou," she said, "and a jet necklace of fake rubies and the earrings Sandy Calder made for me. I remember walking into my bedroom to find my painter friend Bill crying his heart out. He was going to kill himself—some maudlin nonsense about flesh and the devil and a student from Bard College. Instead, he entered a monastery and disappeared from the face of the earth. Didn't we roll up the rug and make a space to dance in? Wasn't there an orchestra?"

"You and Truman," I said, "were the only ones who seemed to know what a fox-trot was."

"All dead and gone," she said. "No one knows what *fun* is anymore."

On the day I was to leave Venice for Paris and a luncheon date with Alice Toklas, Truman brought a copy of *Local Color* to Harry's and inscribed it for me. "My prettiest book," he said, "inside and out. Maybe because I got the most kick out of describing things without having to pretend I've made them up . . . not things so much, as atmosphere. Read first the piece about my train ride in Spain . . . the butterflies."

We walked to my hotel where, as I finished packing, he sat on the edge of the bed.

"When will you be coming home, Truman?"

"Not for years," he said. "Whatever for?"

Back in Taormina for the winter, he did not write until late in January, when I had moved from a house in Westport to an apartment in Cambridge, Massachusetts. "I'm just back from a wintry week in Venice," he said, "so beautiful, a little snow falling on the Grand Canal, San Marco vast and empty, a great burst of warmth when you enter Harry's Bar. I should be sending a gaudy postcard of Venice-by-night, but a letter is best, for I have things to mention. It is almost full spring here in Sicily; the slopes of the village awash with almond blossom, days when we can even have lunch on the terrace with the sea below sparkling like mica.

"You'll be pleased to hear that I'm well toward the end of my book, perhaps even closer. If I am very patient and can keep to routine, I should write the last page by early summer. I don't mean that, since I've always got the last page written before the first one. What I mean is, the last page in the *process*.

"Is it too late for little me to be part of the Poetry Center's next season? I'd like so much to. Should there be a chance, let me know. I have the most stunning new suit (olive velvet, of a kind that *glows)* and I *must* have some place to show it off."

Glad to be able to add his name to the events of the upcoming season, I wrote to tell him so, only to learn he'd changed his mind.

"Well, dear heart," he wrote. "I am not coming home after all. I have given into popular demand—namely, that I do not ever again set foot on American soil. The decision is no hardship, because I never *did* want to come back, and now I'm happy to know I don't have to.

"About June, I'm delighted to think that you will be here— meaning Italy and either of two possibilities: If we're not in residence in Taormina, we will be in some all-by-itself *piccolo palazzo* in Venice. In either case, promise that you will come."

A chance to stay at Yaddo again made me defer plans for Europe until late summer when, instead of visiting Truman in Italy, I meant to spend some time with Dylan Thomas in Wales.

"*Drear* one," wrote Truman, "you *are* a creature of habit—and pretty tiresome habits they are. Yaddo, Y-a-a-d-d-o through time and tide. Haven't you had enough of carbuncular poets, limp ladies scrawling biographies of obscure composers, hairy novelists from the stockyards? I think you are in mortal danger. You will end up as one of those graveyard ghosts who float from one writers' colony to another and only materialize in some bottom-of-the-page obituary.

"All the same I can't wait to see your sweet lollipop face. Which is to say you must come to Venice before July 25th."

On that day I was in London, lunching with my new friend Edith Sitwell and, at midnight, boarding a Third Class sleeper for Wales and Dylan's house in Laugharne. Truman and I would not meet again until October when, once more, he was by himself in Brooklyn

—not in the neighborhood he'd known, but in an old Brooklyn Heights residence a friend of his had converted into apartment units. Ostensibly, this move was undertaken to provide him with working space not available in Jack's cookie-jar flat, and with a base of operations for those sorties into Manhattan nightlife for which Jack had little inclination. But he was often at Jack's. And there we'd have pot-au-feu dinners, get expansive on Chianti, make plans (inevitably canceled) for Christmas on Sanibel Island, Easter on Capri, and dream of other places in the sun that might support cottage industry. One evening over drinks and the sounds of Mabel Mercer I learned Truman had set his sights on Broadway and that he thought he could accomplish this goal with a dramatic version of the novel he had published earlier that year, *The Grass Harp*.

Until the mid-March opening of the play in Boston, everyone held his hand but no one could warm it. When the rough course was run, a single performance stood out: his own. Dressed in Sicilian velvet, he gave a reading of the script to a hard-boiled band of angels in someone's Fifth Avenue apartment, and got his backing on the spot. Staying with it through every rehearsal, he began to regard the man directing it as diabolical and fought with him to save its soul. He rewrote it, got Cecil Beaton to design and dress it, Virgil Thomson to provide incidental music, Mildred Natwick to play the leading role. He went to Boston with it, back to New York with it, and, as far as I could tell, came out of the experience not one whit wiser than he was at the moment of its conception.

The career of *The Grass Harp* was a paradigm and, to someone of Truman's gifts, should have been a warning: Inflated, tricked out, and played for laughs, a gentle lyric conceived in the checkered shade of a remembered childhood was too frail a thing to survive the impositions of show biz razzmatazz. Such were my thoughts (soon to be echoed by every critic in Boston and New York, with the eloquent exception of Brooks Atkinson) on the night when, three blocks from the Colonial Theater where the play had just expired, I sat in the mortuary silence of the Ritz bar with Truman and some of his stoic friends: Jack, Cecil Beaton, Jane Bowles, and a woman crusader against alcohol named Marty Mann. When I turned to wave a last good night to Truman as he sat in the pink glow of that Louis Quatorze setting, I would not have believed it would be another year and a half before I'd see him again or that, when I did, he'd be adrift in a rowboat in the Tyrrhenian Sea.

Since his name now turned up in the papers as frequently as the Duke of Windsor's, I did not have to depend on him to know where he was or what he was doing. *How* he was, I had to interpret from the remarks of friends, most of whom seemed eager to remove the scales from my eyes: "I'm just back from Rome," wrote one of these, "where by chance I saw Truman C one evening on the via Veneto. He sat there, enormously fat, cuddling a scrunchy dog, looking and talking like some defrocked monsignor from Des Moines, and generally acting as though everyone was fascinated by everything he was doing, which they weren't. The picture, I can assure you, was not pretty. How have you put up with such megalomania all these years? If there were an annual award for the Monster American, he'd win this year's, hands down."

"A bolt from the blue!" wrote Truman in answer to a note I'd sent in care of his publishers. "Actually, I've meant to write you for months (and months) but we have been so *mouvementé*, to understate, that it hardly ever seemed the right moment. However, we have settled in Portofino for the summer—and I am catching my breath. You would love Portofino, or do you know it? I am finishing a play, and a story, but how I ever reach the point of finishing *any*thing is beyond me.

"But we don't know your news and you don't know ours; and I want to—know your news, I mean. I've had a curious winter in

Rome and in London—part of it spent making a movie with John Huston—the whole thing was kind of fun and the picture, *Beat the Devil,* is at least the camp of all time. Other than that have been working on the above-mentioned.

"Is there any chance you will be coming to Italy this summer? Malcolm, why haven't you written us?"

To redress, I wrote at once and received in reply a letter from Portofino on stationery filched from Claridge's. "I was touched, relieved, and worried by your sweet note today," he wrote. "Worried because of what you say about your health. I hope (so much) that you are feeling better now, and that there will be no delay in your trip. Because by all means you must come to stay with us in Portofino. It is very charming; the swimming is wonderful—we will be here until September 3rd. Please let us know, with some degree of accuracy, when to expect you."

I named the date, sailed for Spain to experience for myself what it was in Granada that marked a turning point in the writing career of Gertrude Stein, and took the *Andrea Doria* on to Genoa and a taxi to Portofino, where I found, as my journal tells me,

no Truman, because he's not returned from a masked ball in Venice.

"You get the picture," says Jack. "He's following a conga line in the Palazzo Labia, I'm boiling an egg and slicing a salami under that 10-watt bulb. He's shuttling between the Gritti and the Excelsior in the Contessa Volpi's Chris-Craft, I'm taking the dogs to piss on every pillar and post from here to the bus stop. *'Il uomo degli cani,'* they call me, Christ knows what else."

As the dogs, alert for their supper, watch his every movement, the *padrona* comes by with a handful of letters, all of them for Truman. Late sun puts reflections from the marina on the ceiling.

"Well," says Jack, "let me feed these creatures. Looks

like we're on our own. How about a Manhattan? I've got the record to go with it."

"And tell me what street, compares with Mott Street, in July," sings Lee Wiley. I make drinks. The mood of things begins to change.

"You miss New York, Jack?"

"Every other day. Maybe only the idea of it."

"What about Truman?"

"I don't think," he says. "If he does—whenever he does —it's his father and Nina. He's more tied in with that than he ought to be, but it's a fact. Truman needs some kind of family. Too bad that's the only one he's got."

"I'll take Manhattan, the Bronx and Staten . . . Island, too. It's lovely going through the zoo," sings Miss Wiley.

"Let's go down to the hotel," says Jack. "It's their night for *zuppa di pesce.* If we get a table outside, we can see Truman when he comes."

But our evening passes without him. Jack's gloom is Sibelian. We part early.

Ready for bed, I turn out the light, go to the window. Truman's description of the place is apt; I could be peering through a backdrop for *Cavalleria Rusticana.* Among the few souls still abroad in the piazza is Jack, leading the dogs.

8.31.53   Out early, I order an espresso, listen to Sunday bells, watch shopkeepers putting out racks of beach gear, Roman stripes, gimcrack ceramics. At the flat Jack's in shorts and a straw hat, mixing something in a bowl. We'll make a little *giro,* he says, around the headland to San Fruttuoso, a pebble beach where we won't be swamped by trippers down from Genoa. We load picnic supplies into a motorboat.

As we skid across the bay, the dogs stand at the prow

like figureheads. Slowing down off San Fruttuoso, we can see that the Genoese have got there first. The beach is crowded with families under impromptu tents of poles and blankets, or gathered on the shady side of beached fishing boats. It's impossible to lie or sit on the hot melon-size stones for more than a minute. Portable radios squawk and screech, beach balls whizz overhead. The effluvia of blood sausage and purple onion tincture the Sabbath air. We make the best of it for an hour, then agree we've had it.

But the outboard motor won't turn over. Jack yanks until his arms are limp. Dogs yap, children shout advice, whole families, masticating in unison, watch us with sorrowing indifference. There's a shed at the end of the beach housing fishing craft and outboards. Jack tries to find help there. No luck. He comes back to say they're sending for a mechanic who lives halfway up the slope.

Since this man may not come for hours, Jack suggests I find a seat on the *motoscafo* about to make the run to Portofino. I'm reluctant, but he insists. Truman can't bear to come back to an empty house, he says, someone ought to be there.

I'm in the prow, studying the blue mountains beyond Rapallo when I spot a lone figure in a drifting rowboat: Truman. As the *motoscafo* cuts a swath through the still water, I wave my arms and shout over the spray. He waves back, motions toward the shore, begins to row. Disembarked, I wait at the landing.

"Where *were* you?" He pulls up the oars. "Where is everybody? There was no sign of life, anywhere." He tethers his boat to the quay, steps out, gives me a damp hug.

When we've gone halfway across the piazza, I become aware of someone bearing down on us. Slightly bent, this figure is wearing espadrilles, crisply pressed British officers' shorts, a white shirt.

"Truman! What luck to find you off the bat!"

"*Hel*-lo, Noël. Someone told me you'd be coming."

As I'm wondering what's behind the distinctly cool edge to Truman's greeting, we find chairs on a *caffè* terrace and order Cinzanos.

"I'm with Rex and Lilli," says Coward. "The house is rather *up*." He points to the slope opposite the Hotel Splendido. "This is my first stroll out. I hadn't imagined the place so small, but dear me it is entrancing."

His survey takes in the facades of boutiques and the sailing craft tied up at the seawall.

"Look—nannies in their Liberty blouses and plimsolls." He indicates two middle-aged gentlemen in canvas chairs on the afterdeck of a yawl. "East Grinstead, my dear, East Grinstead. What led you to this astonishing place, Truman?"

"Some people in Rome," says T. "They had the flat two summers ago."

"You came, sight unseen?"

"They had photographs."

"Nothing would do it justice, I suppose—the relations of things are so intimate and unexpected."

Coward looks over his shoulder: Half a dozen other people are out in the midday sun—a long-haired girl squinting into a Michelin guide; one fiftyish Italian in a beige silk suit; another in blue jeans and a shirt printed with a nautical symbol under letters spelling St.-Tropez; three Scandinavians, the tallest of whom could be Leif Eriksson. "Well!" he says. "This *is* the place. But I dare not linger." He drains his aperitif. "The Harrisons are termagants about dining hours and there's still that fearful climb, in the jeep. Truman, my cherub, when can we meet?"

"Can you come to dinner? I live up there."

Coward raises his eyes to the flowerpots lined up on the

window ledges of Casa Capote. "I'd adore to, darling, but I'm promised to the Luces and one simply doesn't say no to Madam Ambassador."

"When did *they* get here?"

"This morning, I believe. They're on a yacht." He points toward the marina. "The enormous one, with the limousine cradled on deck, wouldn't you know. Perhaps I could come by be*fore* dinner? About seven?"

He comes at seven, accompanied by a lady friend whose banalities, delivered nonstop and with an air of intellectual audacity, drive us to the windows, gasping for air.

"Look"—Coward is leaning, as I am, on a windowsill —"that sensational black one. It belongs to Arturo Lopez."

We watch the sleek craft head for open water.

". . . of course, when *that* happened," continues the voice behind us, "I knew it was time to call a halt. I don't mind being *used,* I can tell you, that's all part of the game, isn't it? But I do mind being expl*oit*ed and that's the difference between the way we do things in D.C. and the way they do things here. . . ."

We keep to the windows, like people in a burning building.

"Noël," the voice says, finally, "we must bid these charming people good-bye. The launch will be waiting."

She wraps a filmy scarf about her neck. Half a dozen bracelets shimmy to the wrist of the hand she holds out to me. "I've so much enjoyed talking with you," she says.

By the time she has gone like a diminishing echo, we are plopped in chairs, shoes off. "I can't face it," says Truman. "That woman has undone me."

"Can't face what?" says Jack.

"I can't face pounding out one more quivering slab of *vitello.* Let's splurge, let's dine as God meant us to."

The restaurant he chooses is a hanging garden above

the marina, open to the night air, which suddenly contains a rumor of autumn. When I see him shiver, I take off my jacket and put it over his shoulders. He starts to fish in the pockets.

"Hands off," I tell him. But he's already extracted the postcards I've written.

"Postcards are open letters," he says. "I want to know what you're saying about me."

"What if I've said nothing about you?"

"I wouldn't believe it."

"Believe what you want to believe," I tell him, and concentrate on the *piatto di giorno* as if it were a late canto of Ezra Pound's.

Midnight. Sodium light on the pastel facades makes them all of one pockmarked color. Jack has turned in. Truman and I are having a nightcap at a *caffè* when Coward approaches from the waterside, alone.

"That woman—heaven preserve us," he says. "I had no idea what I was about to inflict upon you. May I sit down?"

"What was your dinner like?" asks Truman.

"Torture, at first, exquisite and Chinese. Then Madam Clare began to speak . . . over her, under her, and straight through her. The rest of us took courage. But Clare, I'm afraid, tends rather to mind her tongue in front of Henry. I thought it touching, actually. One doesn't somehow think of her as a wife, anyone's."

This is the end of his report. What he really wants to talk about is writing, Truman's. "You know, I *adore* what you've done," he says, "that extraordinary way you have of putting a fantastic edge on perfectly ordinary things. How do you do it? In the course of a working day, for example, when in your mind you're not seeing anything unusual at all. Do you plan for it? Does it simply *come?*"

Truman gives him an impassive glance. "If it's there *to*

(See detail on the following page.)

come, I suppose. I don't go chasing it with a net. I don't add it to anything. I mean, I don't *add* it as you'd add an ingredient to soup. What else do you want me to say?"

"Nothing you don't care to say, my dear. But in spite of the widespread impression that there's nothing to support the notion, you and I know there's something called the professional secret. And the reason it re*mains* secret is because no one believes it, even when, as you and I might expect, it's spelled out for fair. All I'm asking is, what's yours?"

Truman takes a sip, looks toward the water, from which comes an undercurrent of several kinds of music.

"Well . . . *if*," he says, "*if* I have this way . . ."

We wait for the pronouncement.

"Whatever it is, it's not worth talking about."

Coward turns to me. "*You* know what I mean. It's not an unforgivable thing to ask, now, is it?"

"Truman knows exactly what you're saying," I tell him, "but he wants to let on he doesn't."

(Under his breath, Truman sings, *"Hair is curly, teeth are pearly. You're some ugly chile."*)

"The thing he's afraid of," I continued, "and God knows why, is what he's got most of: animal intelligence, about the way people think, what they exist for, how they scheme to keep themselves alive. So far, those things don't show much in his books. Most people don't suspect they're even there, like some secret he's willing to be found out in but won't himself do anything to assert. He's afraid of it because he doesn't want to be responsible for it. He wants to walk a tightrope, spin glass."

(*"Is it Granada I see,"* sings Truman, *"or only Asbury Park?"*)

"There's a question: How can you continue to be the Venetian glass nephew if it should get about that your real gift is horse sense?"

Bored, or pretending to be, Truman goes on humming to himself. Our conversation, as Coward recognizes, has nowhere to go.

Later, walking back, I tell Truman he's been rude, that Coward had said nothing to warrant such abrupt dismissal.

"Ho . . . hummmm," he says. "The sad old dear, why should I tell *him* anything?"

9.1.53 Less crotchety, I hope, Truman leaves his typewriter midmorning and suggests we go for a swim. Half a mile out into the waters of the Tyrrhenian, he cuts the motor. Legs and arms dangling, we drift and talk—about money, his money, because he's come to the point, he says, when he won't have any.

"Didn't that movie with John Huston bring you a pretty penny?"

"A small fortune," he says, "and it's gone. My father convinced me he needed it. He was, as they say, sliding into bankruptcy. God knows what else, Nina the way she is."

"All of it?"

"Every last dollar."

"Wasn't that being generous to a fault?"

"Maybe. Oh, what the hell. I'm not out for stars. When do you get a chance to do a good deed that *is* a good deed? He's a proud man. I had it, he knew I had it. He's been good to me, a far sight better than my real father ever was."

The surrounding mountains are clear and grainy, like stones under a magnifying glass. I feel I'm afloat in the center of a brimming cup.

Truman asks, perhaps dutifully, about Dylan. I tell him I'm on my way to Wales with one purpose—to dissuade him from making another American tour.

"I'd hope so," he says. "More than one person has told me you carry him around on a lettuce leaf. Haven't you found out what those grubbing English writers are like?"

"Dylan's a Welshman."

"No difference. They go from the nipple to the bottle without changing diapers. Why spend half your life taking care of someone whose mind is on nothing but a pint of beer and a piece of tail? Why should you join a poor man's pub crawl to the grave?"

"Dylan's not poor. He makes more money than I do, a lot more."

"All the more reason to quit playing wet nurse to an overgrown baby who'll destroy every last thing he can get his hands on, including himself."

I don't *have* to, I tell him. In this case, I've wanted to. But no more.

"I'll believe that a month from now."

A speedboat careens across our prow and leaves us rocking.

"You know what your trouble is, Malcolm?"

"Besides ulcers, poverty, stupidity?"

"I'm dead serious. The sad and undeniable thing about you is: You'd rather be a martyr than a success."

Back on even keel, we drift with currents in the changing view.

"I've got a chance to turn 'House of Flowers' into a musical," he says. "The hard part is, once you start working, once I start working, on something that can't ever be my own, I lose touch with the part that *is* my own, like bad money driving out good."

"Why do you do it, then?"

"Opportunities come along," he says. "There's a lot of that bad money involved, or the promise of it. Why not? Doesn't your Dylan Thomas spend time on lots more things than poetry? Documentaries? BBC programs? Didn't I even read that he has a play?"

Through sailing craft at anchor, we reach the seawall, cross to an outdoor place for lunch. Coward, the most elegant of white hunters in buckled khaki shorts and silk fly-button shirt, comes by. We pull up a chair. Truman tells him I'm en route to Wales.

"Wales!" he says. "There's precious little sun in Wales. Come to Jamaica, do what I do. The minute I get to my dear Blue Harbour, I put a shroud over the typewriter and anything else that suggests work and mesmerize myself— for five full days I bake like a lizard in the sand. It's an initiation, a conversion. Then I ignore the sun and get on with it. Oh, except for what you might call a little cosmetic refreshment, say half an hour after breakfast. In fact, my house is for sale. You can buy it this minute. For a bolt-hole, it's perfect."

Truman turns to me. "There's your chance," he says.

"You mean, 'Daylight come and me wanna go home'?"

"Isn't it heaven, Port Maria?" says Coward. "Those green bluffs dropping to the water? I'm told your angelic countrymen are willing to pay a smashing price merely because it's my home. I can't find it in my heart to deny them."

Catching sight of the Harrisons outside a shop, he rises. "Bless me," he says, "I must be off. I told Rex and Lilli I'd be home before they were. So it must be—*arrivederci.*"

Soon it's time for my own departure. Truman drives me to the station in Santa Margherita in the midget convertible he keeps in a garage nearby. "Poor Noël," he says, "he wants to be historical and he knows how ephemeral his sort of thing is. I wish you'd have found a chance to mention his 'contribution to the theater' or something high-sounding like that. I tend to take him for granted. He feels it."

My train for Paris slides in.

"When you coming home, Truman?"

"Not until I absolutely have to, maybe tomorrow."

From the compartment window I see him as he was seven years ago: a chunky kid in T-shirt and shorts, alone in a crowd, glasses pushed up to his forehead, waving good-bye.

"Was delighted, and startled," he wrote three weeks later, "to have your letter this morning: It seems as though you were here only a weekend ago—now you are back in Boston or Connecticut or New York: wherever it is you *do* live. Perhaps it's only that time is so peculiar here—it's beautiful now, the piazza deserted and the sea like 'shook foil.' I have been working very well (for a change). . . .

"The dogs are full of fleas—we've spent all morning bathing them in some odd South African ointment. We still have no *carnet* for the car—heaven knows how we'll leave here, or when. Not until the middle of October, in any event.

"I hope you had a good time at Château Frontenac; you *do* go to the damnedest places—I wonder if anyone has ever had, over a protracted period, a more extraordinary love life: possibly Marilyn Monroe.

"Had a fine offer last week from Carol Reed to do a film script for *A High Wind in Jamaica.* Does it make you happy to learn that I turned it down?

"It was wonderful seeing you, having you here—I always love you very much. Write me."

They would be soon leaving Portofino. "I think for St. Moritz," wrote Truman, "(from sea to snow). I have finished *House of Flowers* and am waiting to hear about the composer, etc. You will be rather amazed when you hear who it is—someone I know you love, but would not associate with me. A very good choice, I think—though it may seem odd at first. I won't tell you, because I'm not sure about it.

"The weather here is wonderful—Jack still goes swimming, but I've given it up. Am sharpening my ice skates instead."

Truman's skepticism about my efforts with Dylan Thomas was well-founded, his prophecy fulfilled. When Dylan came to New York in October, he concealed from anyone who might have helped him the fact that he was seriously ill, and died in just the way physicians in England had told him he would. Truman had no knowledge of this when, in November, he wrote from Switzerland that he was "snowbound in the Alps—it is true—the earliest snowstorm in Swiss history and *we* have to get bogged down in it." Learning of Dylan's death when he got to Paris, he wrote me a consoling note at once: "It was tragic to hear of Dylan's death, and I know how much it must have affected you. I thought of you often during those days, and realized what an infinite, and sad number of arrangements you must have had to make. So of course I understand why you had not answered my letters—but I wish that I could hear from you now.

"I'm not enjoying Paris greatly—and it's in any event such a difficult place in which to work."

Acknowledging my bereavement, he was unaware that he was about to undergo a bereavement of his own.

To come to grips, perhaps to peace, with the fact of Dylan's death, I got away as soon as I could and spent weeks alone on an island in the Bahamas. Back in New York by early January, I went to the Drake Hotel to keep a luncheon appointment with Carson McCullers.

"Bad news," she said, "Nina Capote has killed herself. Truman's come flying back from Paris."

I went to a phone in the lobby; his line was busy. When I'd left the table to call several times without success, Carson suggested I come with her, to Gypsy Rose Lee's, where she was a house guest, and phone Truman from there. Leaning heavily on her cane, she followed me out to the street. I had to all but lift her bodily into a taxi.

"Is it 153 East 63rd Street," she said aloud, "or 351?"

The driver, swiveling, gave us a hard, flat glance and drove to 153.

"I think this is it," said Carson, "I seem to remember the door."

Inside, as bursts of typewriter clatter resounded from the floor above, she settled herself at a table in an alcove that had walls painted, and boldly signed, by Vertès. Nodding at the ceiling, she said: "Gypsy. Another novel. She'll be down when the kid gets home from school. If you go into the kitchen and open the end cabinet, you'll find my private supply of J. W. Dant. There's a wall phone you can use. Tell Truman to call when he'd like to talk."

Truman's voice was weary. He'd be staying at the apartment with his father; he was concerned about me. Some of the stories he'd heard about Dylan's death were "truly morbid." I told him not to believe them, that the truth was bad enough. He said he'd phone when the situation at home was clear.

I took Carson her drink. "What did he say?" she asked. "Did he sound sad or did he sound relieved?"

"Sad."

"Did you mention me?"

"No."

"Just as well," she said. "He's mad at me. He accuses me of making trouble and then leaving it. He just can't stand the idea that I knew Newton long before he did."

This was the first indication I'd had that the intimacy Truman shared with Carson was uneasy, my first sense of the twin-star magnetism that held them suspended in a state of infantile belligerence.

In Truman's eyes, Carson's physical disabilities were aspects of self-indulgence and not the intimations of mortality her early death would confirm. Carson was "getting away with it," he thought, even when it was obvious that her figure grew more frail and that her attempts to handle the simple demands of daily existence were ever more slow and painful. So it was no surprise to find that his view of my budding friendship with Mrs. McCullers was both wry and cautionary.

"You'll be trapped there, and then enslaved," was his only comment when I told him some time later that I was seriously thinking of an invitation to join her in South Carolina. And when, from time to time, I'd report having lunched with her, or escorted her to a party, his response was succinct: "Watch out. Carson has an instinct for people like you—a killer instinct."

Disregarding his advice, I continued to take delight in his waiflike friend and, in the course of things, to persuade her to make an appearance at The Poetry Center. The appointed date, according to my journal, was May 8, 1954.

Since she must walk with a cane, Carson has asked friends who live not far from The Poetry Center to give her supper. When I get there, she's huddled in a big chair, curled in on herself like a snail. She holds out a cold hand.

"I'm scared, all over," she says. "Will there be a lot of people?—like those who come for Edith Sitwell and Truman?"

"A lot."

With a look of spiritual bedragglement, she snuggles deeper into her chair. "Does Truman *act* his stories or just read them? I'll bet he shows off. Am I right?"

Tennessee comes over, a plate of food in his hand.

"Tenn, honey," she says. "I just can't eat a thing. I'm too *scared.*"

"Come on, now," he says. "Be a good girl. Sit up and eat your food."

Like a compliant child—aided by a very dark mixture of Jack Daniel's and ice—she does what he asks.

"John Malcolm," she says, "I have this idea . . . would it be all right if Tenn came on stage with me? I mean, if he just *sat* there?"

"That's a very silly idea, Carson," says Tennessee. "People are coming to see *you,* goosey."

"John Malcolm? . . . it would be all right?"

Tennessee shakes his head and rolls his eyes, but only for my benefit. I can tell this is but a preface to surrender. An hour later they take the stage together . . . to gasps of surprise and renewed waves of applause as recognition of Tennessee becomes general. They sit at a table equipped with microphones, take an amused look at the dimly lighted audience, then bend their heads in conference.

By giving all of his attention to her as she begins to read, Tennessee quietly commands Carson's listeners to do likewise. But he is unable to resist the avuncular smiles that overtake him at certain passages, or to suppress a series of infectious giggles. When, finally, he laughs out loud, so does the audience. Carson lifts her head, as if to learn what all the commotion is about.

When I reported the occasion to Truman, and asked that he return a clipping I'd sent him, his response was minimal: Honey—

Here you is—though by the time it's my turn I, too, shall probably have to walk on stage assisted by a cane and Signor Williams.

Jack has gone to Vermont but I am stuck right here so call me if you come to town.

Love

T.

Two weeks later he phoned me at my office. He was having some people in that night, he said, after the late show at a nightclub called the Latin Quarter. I must come.

"But," he said, "first you have to guess who the party's *for.* "

"Garbo?"

"Not her kind of thing."

"Isak Dinesen? Billie Holiday?"

"Not even close. Christine, she's an absolute dear."

"Christine who?"

"Jorgensen.* Actually, she's sort of heartbreaking, but spunky, too. You'll understand when you see her. Call for me here around eleven."

The program that evening at the Poetry Center was a joint reading by Richard Wilbur and Richard Eberhart. As soon as the doors were open, I could see that their presence in New York had attracted so many old friends of theirs and mine that the occasion took on the feeling of a class reunion. At a reception afterward, I forgot about Truman until midnight, when I phoned to tell him I wouldn't be coming to his party.

"Why *not?*" he said. "What's so scintillating where *you* are?"

Poets, I told him, old friends.

"Malcolm, my pet"—the acid in his voice would melt wire— "that's cornball stuff. You goin' be one li'l cornball *all* your life?"

"Probably."

"All I have to say is this: You *be* there, hear?" The phone clicked.

When I got to the Latin Quarter about one, the maître d' took me to a big round table where three people were already seated—Donald Windham; a woman I recognized as the comedienne Alice Pearce; a man I didn't know. Truman came in with Judith Anderson,

---

* The ex-G.I. whose Scandinavian sex-change operation was a cause célèbre taken up by the tabloid press with headline coverage unequaled since.

Jane and Paul Bowles, and Oliver Smith. The overture to the late show precluded conversation.

Miss Jorgensen, as thin as a coatrack on which someone had hung an evening gown, came out singing "Getting to Know You" in a half-croaking voice and moved through an upsy-daisy patty-cake-man choreography on high heels that seemed about to collapse. This was followed by other numbers chosen, apparently, to suit an androgynous register. Bizarre and pathetic, the performance was finally inoffensive, almost winning in its bravery against odds.

In a babushka and a camel's hair wraparound coat, sniffling into a balled-up handkerchief, Miss Jorgensen joined our table. She'd caught this awful cold, she said. Perhaps we could tell by her voice? Nevertheless, she told us, the management was thinking of extending her engagement if, that is, she would agree to a cut in salary.

A hand loaded with rings reached across to hers and covered it firmly.

"My dear," said Judith Anderson. "An artist never, *nev*er agrees to a reduction in salary. It is undignified, it is unnecessary. I speak as one who has every reason to know." With an air of unchallenged rectitude, she surveyed the room and lifted her crème de menthe. Miss Jorgensen stared.

Libby Holman and Montgomery Clift were on the way, Truman told us. When they got here, we'd all go on to his place.

"Gosh," said Miss Jorgensen, "I'm plumb sorry as anything, but I can't go anywhere tonight." She fished a second damp handkerchief out of a pocket. "The only place for this little girl is bed."

Called to the phone, Truman came back to say that the others had given up. Suddenly bored by his sniffling star and the petering out of everything else, he called for the check.

"She's even sadder than I thought," he said as we settled into a taxi. "Six months, she'll be playing carnivals."

Asleep in Truman's guest bed, I was awakened by the sounds of something being munched on. The night-table clock said 3:06. All the lights were on. Truman was sitting up, newspapers all about him, poking fragments of peanut brittle into his mouth as he perused the gossip column of the *Daily Mirror.*

"Want to see an item," he said, "about yours truly?"

I put a pillow over my head.

"Mail it to me."

As Truman began to assume the role of mascot to café society, we began to drift farther apart. Since the friends we shared were few, and the people he was coming to know belonged to that channel of New York life where art, high fashion, and big money flow together, our common ground was shrinking. On winter mornings when, waking late, he'd be scanning the papers to see what Cholly Knicker-bocker or Leonard Lyons had to say about him, I'd be scanning lecture notes on Emily Dickinson or Hart Crane in the halls of the University of Connecticut nearly two hundred miles away. When we did meet, the occasion was apt to be one at which, like a country cousin or, as he once put it, "family," I'd be dutifully asked to come along.

One of these, costing me a night's sleep, nevertheless afforded me a glimpse into that world in which, I thought, he was permanently sealed—only to recognize later that it was but a way station on the road to Maecenas' eyrie on his Esquiline hill and Jay Gatsby's pad in West Egg.

Like his first reading at The Poetry Center, Truman's second was sold out in advance, to no one's surprise, least of all his. But some-how this did not bolster his confidence or inure him to the intense stage fright that always seemed at odds with his temperament. When I reached the Green Room, his eyes were as frightened as a lost dog's, his hands sweaty cold.

"You're seeing the last of me," he said.

"How so?"

"I'm going back to Paris. Jack's still in the hotel there, with the dogs. He's had it, he says, and I can't blame him. Listen, there's a party afterwards you have to come to."

"Tonight?"

"It's Harold Arlen's birthday."

"I have a class to teach at eight in the morning, five hours from here."

His eyes narrowed. "I happen to know," he said, "that teaching school in the sticks has not prevented you from enjoying certain other entertainments I could mention."

After the reading—another virtuoso performance that began in a low key and ended in clamor—Truman went ahead while I stayed in my office for an hour of paperwork. Then, the only thing on my mind was what I was going to say about Herman Melville to my eight o'clock class, most of whom were already asleep in their dormitory beds. It was midnight when I got to Harold Arlen's. A bushy-haired man showed me where to put my coat—on a bed on which lay the playwright William Inge, sound asleep. "Bill's resting, if you know what I mean," said the bushy-haired man. "I'm a stranger here myself—George Kaufman."

As we shook hands, Truman appeared. "Anyone you'd like to meet right off?"

I told him I'd like a drink and he showed me where to get it. When I could look around, I first noticed Jack's ex-wife sprawled against a mound of pillows and looking rather like one of the "French dolls" the girls of 1925 kept on their beds. Thin and bony— she would die of cancer within the year—she smiled a detached smile and lit a black cigarette with a gold tip. Standing at the end of the sofa was Marlene Dietrich, encircled by the arms of Montgomery Clift. Mutually transfixed, they appeared to exchange monosyllables now and then, but for the most part simply stood there, staring into one another's eyes. Dietrich was wearing something less like fabric than molten silver. Clift's suit was too big for him; he seemed to have shrunk in it. Very slowly and deliberately, they would kiss, holding one another like praying mantises.

A second drink and I knew I'd missed my last train. Giddy in the prospect of a night without sleep, I moved toward Janet Flanner— the only person there, excepting Truman, with whom I'd previously exchanged as much as a word. But at that moment Harold Arlen sat down at the piano and the room froze. He had a new song for us, he announced, a song for "Judy's" next picture. In a voice that scratched at every phrase, he began his ballad of the man that got away. In the echoed bravos and long applause that followed, I found Truman at my side.

"Having a good time?" he asked.

"There *is* someone I'd like to talk with," I said. "Janet Flanner."

"Suivez-moi."

But we did not make it through the crowd. Abe Burrows had replaced Arlen at the piano and *his* show had begun. "What you all want to hear?" he called, and sent a ripple across the keyboard. "What you all want Abie to play?"

Dietrich's voice rang out. "The Holland song, Abe, play the Holland song!" To a general murmur of approval, Burrows ran his chubby fingers over the keys once more. *"Why don't the boys,"* he sang, and made googly eyes around the room, *"why don't the boys take their fingers out of the dikes and go"*—a dirty chuckle here— *"and go, and go on home to their girls."*

Dietrich led the applause, urging him into a sequence of his own show tunes, to which, from the moment, no one paid the least attention.

Three-thirty. In the diminished company, Truman sat on the floor, his head against Harold Arlen's knee. The rest of us, a circle of stockinged feet on a coffee table, sipped brandy and waited for someone to say something. Framed in a doorway leading to a library, Dietrich and Clift, stiff and upright as dolls in a box, prolonged their catatonic clinch.

Daylight found me dozing through lower Connecticut on the milk train. By seven-thirty, bending to my notes at the counter of a campus diner, I bit into a powdered doughnut and marked a foot-note: "The incest motive in *Pierre,* for example, might certainly have come to Melville from Webster or Ford, but it is still more reminis-cent of the sentimental, the Gothic, or in general the romantic school." At eight-ten, hangoverish and forgiving, I waited until the latecomers had settled themselves, noisily emptied my pipe into a wastebasket, then began my lecture.

The Grass Harp, its career brief, its succès d'estime modest, never-theless had provided Truman with an entry into the theater. He hoped now to make a more solid place there with his musical com-edy version of "House of Flowers," a short story based on his experi-ences in Haiti. This production was scheduled for the end of the year, most of which Truman would spend abroad and out of range. Except for what I read in the papers and news magazines, I had no word of him, a circumstance that promised to become permanent. Old friends like me were being replaced by show business acquain-tances who, in turn, would soon themselves be displaced as Truman's affections turned to individuals in the international society of the conspicuously rich.

I followed this ascension, if that's what it was, as news services reported it, trying to spot the telling facts embedded in the hype of columnists' fancies. One day's report would have him ensconced like a baby Voltaire in the ateliers of the Ile-de-France; another would have him pillowed on the afterdeck of a Greek shipping tycoon's yacht at anchor off Skyros; still another would have him weekending in this or that great house, jollying up the gentry with his wit and wisdom, playing *charades en travesti,* and otherwise being "seen with."

Crediting no more than half of these reports, I still wondered what had so swiftly deflected Truman's obsession with working space and working hours, an obsession that had governed him through all the years of our acquaintance. Knowing where he was, I could not tell where he was going, and so took comfort in the fact that he had never in his life embarked without a well-calculated destination. Yet what was the purpose of this extended cruise among the Isles of the Blest? His milieu of playwrights, designers, editors, and movie producers had no doubt been a source of professional advantage and of measurable reward. What would he get from the notoriously rich that he wouldn't have to pay for?

Midsummer, he was back in New York and I was bound for Italy and England. On the day before I sailed, we met in the early August hush of the Plaza's Oak Room. Approaching his table, I could feel the weight of his disapproval.

"What's your problem?" I asked.

"Have you never been told, my dear Malcolm, that one never, never wears a bow tie with a button-down collar?"

"I only break the rules I know," I told him. "That's one of them."

Chin in hand, he leaned on the table in a caricature of weariness. "Something wrong?"

"I can't work," he said. "I haven't worked in months, except for the effort of tearing up a novel I'd almost completed. With my two bare hands."

He snapped his swizzle stick in two, then in four. His drink was untouched. "I hope you haven't made plans for dinner," he said. "If I go home, I'm trapped."

After a meal at The Colony, we went on to The Blue Angel. In both places he took the attentions of people who came to our table with an unruffled air of noblesse oblige. Someone told him his movie was "mad, *mad* fun." Someone reported what C.C. said to Boo-boo in the ladies' room at Bergdorf—"actually, she'd had this fainting spell at Ohrbach's and rushed uptown, in case it was serious."

These chirpings were counterpoint. On Truman's mind was a burden of doubt and gloomy self-assessment. Six years into a public career as a novelist, he had begun to lose ground to newer and more robust talents, and to find himself beyond the pale of even those critics who, charitably ignoring the circus tactics of promotion, had once read him soberly and reviewed him favorably. Between the man of letters and the man-about-town, the balance had gone badly out of whack; the boy of shining promise had been overtaken by the boulevardier. Truman understood this, I learned, a little better than I did. Yet his contempt for the world of "serious" literature and its judges remained lively, and his aversion to that kind of academic squalor where the lares and penates are the *TLS* and the diaper pail, the *OED* and the candle in the Chianti jug, was pronounced. But this had not prevented him from reading either those "gray people," as he called them, and their "drab quarterlies," or the collections of literary criticism in which it was essential that, one way or the other, he figure.

Was it already the fact that Truman as a public commodity had caused Truman as a writer to be closed out? Respectful of even the most dronelike of my colleagues, I knew they still made distinctions between aspiration and ambition, genius and talent, achievement and exhibitionism. Within a decade such distinctions would be seriously blurred. But in August 1954, Truman's aesthetic pretensions were fast losing credibility, and he knew it. The portrait of the artist as a precocious Little Lord Fauntleroy had been intriguing, amusing, and acceptable; the portrait of the artist as a lapdog in the salons of Sutton Place and the XVIᵉ Arrondissement was not.

As we were about to leave the nightclub, he took from his pocket a white envelope and handed it across the table. "My little bon voyage present," he said. "Post it the minute you get to Venice." The envelope was addressed:

John Malcolm Brinnin

Miss Katharine Hepburn
Palazzo Poppadopoli
1365 San Polo
Venezia

"You'll love her," he said. "She's staying there with Constance Collier while she makes a movie, about this old maid schoolteacher who goes to Venice and gets laid by Rossano Brazzi. My note says they should ask you to lunch or something, and that's what they'll do."

*H*ouse of Flowers opened at the end of December, went tottering into the new year, and collapsed. Beautiful and vapid, it had too much star-studded weight to carry, too much scenery, by Oliver Messel, to justify, too much business to do in the confines of a creaking veranda in Port-au-Prince. Deserted in midcareer by its original director Peter Brook and by its choreographer George Balanchine, it arrived on Broadway as "an extended vaudeville act," as Truman said later, "for Miss Pearl Bailey."

Truman was not aware that I had attended the opening night, when, three nights later, I waited for him in The Poetry Center's Green Room. Arriving promptly at seven (he had insisted on a rehearsal), he proceeded to take charge of lights, amplifiers, curtains, acoustics. To make sure that just the particularly flattering nuance of pink light would strike his face, just the right shadows, he asked me to assume his place on stage while he studied the effects from different parts of the empty auditorium.

"Pretend you're reading from my book," he called down from the last row. "I want to see how close I can hold it . . . without using my glasses . . . and still show my face."

I followed his directions.

"In your *left* hand," he called. "I want my right one free for gestures."

Impatient with these diddling adjustments, I spoke low enough, or so I thought, to be heard only by stagehands. "Truman, baby," I said, sotto voce, "this ain't *Camille.*"

"Who *said* it wasn't?" Truman called out. "Let me see what happens if you put the mike a little to the left."

Just before curtain time Harold Arlen came backstage, where, from the wings, we listened to Truman's reading and watched his performance. "I love that young man," said Arlen. "One of the most enchanting souls I've ever encountered. He's very fond of you. What's going to become of him?"

A roar of laughter interrupted us. Truman, waiting for quiet, glanced our way.

"Why do you ask?"

"I'm not certain he can take care of all that talent. Are you?"

"I used to be. Now I'm not. . . ."

"But you believe in him."

"In some ways, more than he believes in himself."

My presence at this third reading of Truman's was unofficial—a response to his request that I be "on hand" and that I introduce him. Dylan's death had taken the heart out of any thought of satisfaction I might still obtain from my work at The Poetry Center and I had handed in my resignation months before. No longer a weekly commuter to New York, I now gave my attention to teaching and to writing down memories of Dylan's career in America. By late spring of 1955 it was apparent to my publisher, if not yet to me, that I had the makings of a book. After delivering the manuscript late in July, I went to Europe on a seven-week trip that began and ended in Naples. There I boarded a ship carrying cargo and ninety passengers on a fifteen-day crossing to Hoboken. Leghorn was our first port of call. Next day we docked in Genoa, where, we were told, the ship would remain in port for eighteen hours. Already familiar with Genoa,

whose charms I tended to equate with Buffalo's, I quit the ship, took
a taxi to the *stazione,* a train to Santa Margherita, a bus to Portofino.
The piazza was gray and deserted; unswept leaves lay matted in the
gutters of the colonnade; the boutiques were boarded up; a white
dog on the seawall slept on his paws. Truman was right. The wind
on the marina did give the effect of "shook foil." Sitting down on
one of the few chairs left outside "our" *caffè,* I ordered a negroni.
Looking up, I could see that the windows of Casa Capote were
closed, the geraniums on the sills left to wither.

Saddened by the crepuscular sense of everything, I watched the
skittering leaves, studied the lifeless buildings, then opened the copy
of *Time* I'd brought from the ship. Turning pages without reading
them, I sensed that something had caught my eye. Flipping back, I
saw what it was: Truman, smiling his big baby's smile, dancing in
the arms of Marilyn Monroe. Unprepared for the little bolt of rage
that ran through me, I stared at the marina for one long moment,
then took a postcard from my pocket and, with a pen that crackled,
sent my friend a message. Its burden was simple, designed to scathe:
Was *this* the best hope of American letters? I asked. Was *this* the
Portrait of the Artist as a Young Man? "Joyce's motto was, Silence,
exile, and cunning," I said. "What's *yours?*" and signed it, "Reader
of *Time.*"

Almost tipped from my chair by a rush of wind, I took shelter in
an arcade under scribbles of lightning, buckets of rain. Waiting for
the squall to blow itself out, I put my postcard in a box and, for
emphasis, clicked the lid. A few minutes later the sun came out like
a door opened. Already nibbled by regret, I crossed a pavement
steaming gold and climbed into a bus for Genoa and the long voyage
home.

A moment of outrage had tricked me into the ranks of Truman's
detractors. With time to suffer so hard a fall from grace, I began to
dwell on my apostasy, probe my motives, and to find them without
charity or honor. If friendship had indeed given me prerogatives of

judgment, I should have exercised these long ago, or shut up. Truman was responsible to himself, not to my expectations. The ties that bound us had become a bit thin, but there was still no reason to further raddle them with sarcasm which, I had to recognize, was as much a plea for attention as it was an act of judgment.

His response came in October, when he wrote: "Despite the (to me) startlingly unjust contents of your Portofino card, I hopefully assume it was intended as some sort of good-friend, stern-critic comment. If it was meant otherwise, and your words were weighed, then frankly, dear heart, I don't know what the hell you are talking about. You have, and will always have, a most particular place in my affections. If I have disappointed you as an artist (as you suggest), that is one thing; but certainly as a person, as a friend, I have done nothing to deserve your misguided candor. If memory serves, this is the second time you have rounded on me; on the previous occasion I correctly deciphered the clumsy hand of a malevolent informer. But I am not a detective by profession, and so shall have to leave the clues to this latest attack untraced. However, rest in the knowledge that you are on the popular side; my stock in all quarters is very low, and if the number of folk I have apparently offended were laid end to end they would circle the globe.

"I've had a quiet, working summer. Moreover, I lost thirty pounds: Am just a svelte bag of golden bones. We're going back to the city next week.

"Please consider, and write your perhaps unworthy, but still loving, very loving—T."

This was more than I deserved; and when my memoir of the last years of Dylan Thomas was published in November, his message was among the first to arrive: I THINK YOUR BOOK IS WONDERFUL. LOVE TRUMAN. The telegram itself was an index: Friendship had been reduced to its offices.

That may have been so. But it wasn't long before I came to see his approval in another light and in a different context.

Distant as it seemed, there had been a time when as aspiring writers we stood more or less on common ground, cherished many of the same literary heroes and heroines, and maintained a running dialogue reflecting our concerns about self-definition and the place each of us might find in what was then a still comprehensible "world of letters." But when Truman became "bankable," in the Hollywood sense of the word, and his signature took on the character of a property and purveyable commodity, I could in no way assume our ground was common. The big deals in which he was involved were, to me, remote and exotic transactions. Concerns once shared became independent interests; our common ground was split into islands continually drifting apart.

Truman's unexpected enthusiasm for *Dylan Thomas in America* was genuine, I came to see, simply because that "intimate memoir" was in part a realization of an idea we'd come upon at the same time and which hit us with a surprise we were quick to share. Quite independently, the questions we'd asked ourselves were: Why cannot reportage and other forms of factual accounting be shaped like fiction, charged with the energies of fiction, and so move at the imaginative pace of the best of it? Weren't all good novels themselves full of information? Why did even the most brilliant of nonfiction writers assume their work was in the service of a lesser calling than that which sanctified the most pedestrian of novelists?

In my case, these ideas and their ramifications were at first merely something to entertain until, at leisure, I might explore ways to use them. But in the dispirited aftermath of Dylan Thomas's death they reemerged with enough force to distract me from the conventional biography on which I was at work, and eventually caused me to put that work aside. In a long and desolate period of brooding bewilderment, I lost the thread of Gertrude Stein and was unaware of the fact that I had another, more urgent, "story," until individuals who knew of my involvement with Dylan implored me to tell it. Among these were Edith Sitwell and T. S. Eliot. Edith's encouragement was based in a strong concern that "America"—a catchall in the British press for everything craven and opportunistic—not be made the scapegoat for a death that was, as she well knew, a matter of private devils as relentlessly active in Wales and London as they were in San Francisco and Manhattan. Eliot's was based on a letter I'd written within thirty-six hours of Dylan's passing, acquainting him and his house-mate, John Hayward, with the truth of deathbed events already wildly distorted, particularly in England. Since I had meanwhile come to feel weighted with a burden of knowledge that threatened to become intolerable, these sanctions were a kind of blessing. Accepting them, and ready to act, I still had the problem of how to cast a story which, with a bit of prompting, would tell itself. Recalling my last talks with Truman, I suddenly knew that I had a "nonfiction novel" in the form of a memoir, its continuity predetermined, its climaxes in place and awaiting only the certification of detail. The result was a record of Dylan's last years in an account bordering, for me at least, on an act of exorcism. In the process, what I learned was what I knew: Fiction and nonfiction, categories inextricable in life are, on the page, devices of equal convenience.

Pleased by Truman's recognition of what I had done, I coveted the chance to resume conversations that might now have a less theoretical focus. But our dialogue was over. Discussions on the point would have to remain the last of any literary consequence between us. Soon, island to island, we'd exchange polite inquiries; but we would no longer send messages. Instead of comparing notes and confiding ambitions, we made reports from the field . . . and, as usual, saw to it that these did not interfere with the retailing of urgent gossip.

Nearly ten years had passed since Truman, to the music of harp strings, had stepped into my life, and now I would not see him for three more. Geography was partly responsible for this, but the larger factor was his apparent fascination with a stratum of society whose well-heeled and happy few found him sufficiently astonishing, amusing, and ornamental to take him, as time would bitterly tell, in.

Missing Truman, I could only applaud the success which his failures in the theater did not impede, and observe with some degree of concern his membership, honorary though it might be, in a segment of the population so rarefied as to render him sacrosanct. Still at a point in my life where I did not know that dear friends went away, I had yet to learn that proximity is nine-tenths of friendship, absence the swamp where all the gratuitous bearers of resentment blithely cluster and breed. Without "my" Truman, I began unconsciously to accept the image that belonged to anybody. The fact that I had long since predicted the ultimate disparity of man and mask was of no account and little comfort. Out of touch with one, I was alternatively entertained and appalled by the public parade of the other and, like Harold Arlen, asked myself, What will become of him?

Meanwhile we continued to exist for one another by tokens and missed connections: a postcard, written at a window in Leningrad overlooking the Neva on New Year's Eve; a snapshot of him and a bulldog ("my own *force de frappe*") from Switzerland; a note from Rome. One summer day in London, writing to him in Spain from a room on the second floor of the Connaught Hotel, I did not know that he was at the same moment addressing me in Boston from a room on the third floor of the same hotel.

"What irony!" he wrote from Spain. "I arrived *back* from London three hours ago!

"Am delighted you will soon be in Europe again, and if your

lectures for the State Dept. bring you to London, please ring. Would, bless you, love to have a nice riproaring reunion. I long to see you.

"Meanwhile, be wary of charming student delegations."

Through hit and miss, one thing about him remained constant: his generosity in sharing his friends with his friends. In this, as in his gritty devotion to his work, he operated unobtrusively and pulled strings—making sure that I would meet one of "my best Russian pals" at 1 Pirogovska Street, Odessa; that, when I went to Ireland, I would have a letter of introduction to John ("craggy and funny and wildly intelligent") Huston; that I would call on Adlai Stevenson, "a dear; he brought me a teddy bear all the way from Alaska"; and, hearing I'd be aboard a little ship taking the English novelist Rose Macaulay back to Trebizond, wrote: "I have some friends going on that cruise and I think you will like them: Diana Duff Cooper and Lady Juliet Duff and her son Michael."

One August day aboard the little *S.S. Hermes* docked in Piraeus, I was having a prelunch aperitif with Miss Macaulay when Diana Cooper came into the lounge where we were sitting. Lady Diana was costumed in a closely pleated white skirt, a naval blazer with insignia on its breast pocket, and a cap so heavy with "scrambled eggs" it might have belonged to an admiral. "Rose! Look!" she said as, like a little girl, she spun around to show how her skirt flared out. But Miss Macaulay, peering into a handbook of Mycenaean wall paintings, missed the performance which, in the circumstance, I was left to applaud. At six that evening, after we had all gone our separate ways in Athens, I was handed a note to the effect that Lady Diana Cooper and Lady Juliet Duff would be pleased were I to join them for dinner. Puzzled—I'd been seeing them on land and sea for ten days—I met them, as they had proposed, in the lounge and learned what the sudden formality was all about. "We had tea with Cecil Beaton at the Grande Bretagne," said Lady Diana. "Cecil had a note from Truman Capote, *sternly* instructing him to see that we looked you up. We kept our mouths shut and said we would."

"My son Michael adores him," said Lady Juliet. "Is he really so much the tyrant?"

Responding to a postcard from the Villa Meltemi, Paros, Greece, I told Truman I'd be coming to Europe as soon as I had finished my work with the Ford Foundation, an assignment involving the choice of writers to whom the foundation was about to grant large sums of money. His return letter promised an end to a long breach: He would be giving a reading at The Poetry Center in December, another in Cambridge, for *The Harvard Advocate.*

"Did I tell you," he wrote, "that I have a short novel *[Breakfast at Tiffany's]* coming out in October? Very curious to have your reaction.

"Delighted about your sinecure-sounding Ford Foundation chores. Maybe you can manage to pour some of the gravy on my barren plate. Lord knows no one needs *aid* more than me. We will be here until September 1st. Would love to see you on Paros, but perhaps we will connect in Venice. . . . Anyway, I'm glad to have you back in my life, for you've been sorely missed. Because you know I love you a great good deal. . . ."

To be back in Truman's life, I would soon learn, was simply to be on call; to witness, if not to swell, his progress; to attend far more than to participate. When the editors of the *Advocate* asked me to introduce the reading he was to give in December, I told them he needed no introduction, that my presence on the platform would be supererogatory, and reported as much to Truman.

"On the whole," he wrote from Willow Street, Brooklyn, "I rather wish you would introduce me: it quietens an audience and focuses their attention—last year, at Chicago, they decided not to have an introduction, and I suppose it was 'effective,' but it took me ten minutes to get the audience in a listening mood. However, do what you think best." What I thought best was irrelevant.

His fee for this reading was high, he wrote, "because I *must* stay at the Ritz." But to his dismay, the Ritz would not have him. The reason, according to the management, was simply the unavailability at that time of even a single room. Unwilling to accept this, Truman enlisted a New York friend to make a reservation for the same nights. When this was confirmed at once, Truman had to face up to the fact that, in the innermost temple of the bean and the cod, he was persona non grata.

Without attempting to learn what lay behind the hotel's rejection, I was about to call on the help of an acquaintance highly placed in the State House when Truman himself put an end to the matter. "I doubt that I will get into the Ritz," he wrote, "so will gladly go to the Copley—*if* they will have me.

"I will take a morning train, arriving early afternoon; please *don't* meet me. Will go to the hotel: will you come there at three?"

From the window of his room, I watched dark figures crossing the bird-tracked snow of Copley Square and waited for Truman to emerge from the shower the noise of which, unalleviated by song, had now been drumming for five minutes. Half an hour earlier I had myself crossed the square in a mood of trepidation balanced by curiosity. But this was all dispersed at a glance; three years ago might have been yesterday. I could see that Truman had gained some weight, lost some hair; that he dressed with a conservatism in which I could spot no touch of sartorial heresy. But my deeper curiosity held. He was much richer, I knew, but I wondered if he were wiser. Did his strange turning toward the moneyed and powerful of this world represent merely a sunflowerlike tropism or was it a privileged observer's means of acquisition? "Little T., who—bet your boots— wastes not, wants not," had been his self-characterization twelve years ago. But that was at a time when, overtaken by an illness, he had made a writer's most of it. Could he say as much for something *he* pursued and overtook? The noise of the shower ceased.

"English," he said. The room was suddenly redolent of musk and obscure flora. "I buy it in London, a little shop in Jermyn Street."

Putting on a sort of truncated dressing gown, a black velvet *le smoking* that came barely to his waist, he went to a serving table in a corner and began dropping ice into glasses. "This thing must be seven or eight years old." He fingered a still shiny lapel. "Remember Jack's crazy little apartment . . . that subarctic toilet in the hall? One day . . . I was by myself, in February, I think . . . I was wearing this and nothing else, *noth*ing else, not so much as a ribbon, when I went to the can, pulled the chain . . . remember? . . . and started back into the apartment only to find I'd locked myself out. The hallway was freezing, me in bare feet. What to do? I rapped on doors. Not a peep. Then I went down to that Chinese laundry . . . a sign on the door: owner sick, pick up laundry at some address on Third Avenue. The sidewalk by the schoolyard was full of wet snow, traffic splashing by, people in boots and galoshes. Know what I did? I walked the length of that block, jaybird naked except for this . . . and got to the cigar store on the corner, walked in, borrowed a dime, made my phone call, and went *back* to the place as if I were in no more hurry than someone on the way to the dentist. Scotch?"

I took the drink and bided my time. I had questions for Truman, but not now. The important thing was that the man I knew, coming easily into focus, had sent a hundred published images spinning into a world I didn't know.

We went to the *Advocate*'s cocktail party; we went to dinner at the home of his old friend Frances McFadden, where, in deepest Cambridge, we broke bread with the Robert Lowells and the Mark DeWolfe Howes at a table echoing with a sort of unassignable hilarity. The source of this was an out-of-the-blue declaration by Mark Howe that, try as he might, he found it impossible to suppress a lifelong aversion to Indians. Stunned into silence by this admission from the liberal aristocrat who was the pride of the Harvard Law School, we waited for a sign: Were we being booby-trapped into a joke?

Not at all. The strained silence held; wine was poured with prolonged care and notable delicacy; looks were exchanged—including one between me and Truman, wide-eyed and cautious.

Finally, someone spoke up: "Sheets, you mean? Or feathers?"

Through the gasping laughter that followed, we could hear, like the voice of a drowning man, one last half-stifled shout.

"Sheets! Sheets!"

We repaired to a drawing room with a multipaned window that looked out upon a whited garden. Our brandy glasses reflected the log fire toward which Truman held out his hands. "Come back to the hotel with me," he whispered. "I'm cold all over."

In the taxi I became aware that he was trembling. "You coming down with something?"

"It's been this way for days—fright, like something lurking."

I took off my gloves: "Here, let me rub your hands."

Like a child offering a kitten, he held them out. They were ice-cold.

"That's better," he said, and put on the gloves I no longer needed. In the rearview mirror the driver's eyes met mine, and turned away.

Back in the hotel room he put on his smoking jacket and snuggled into the pillows of a sofa. "Make mine a double," he said as I poured nightcaps. A television set, pictures without sound, caught my peripheral vision but seemed no part of his. "I leave it on for company," he said, "the way kids listen to music they don't hear. *Well.*" He raised his glass. "Here's to Cambridge, and its furnished souls."

"I want to know some things, Truman. Answer me if you want to, don't if you don't."

The look he fixed on me as I took the other end of the sofa was lofty with forbearance.

"You spend half your life these days—more, for all I know—with people who travel in their own sleek planes and their Silver Clouds, who keep empty villas around the Mediterranean, shooting boxes in Argyll, bank accounts in Zurich or Grand Cayman, people who own the earth from which they're insulated as completely as though they lived in time capsules. What's in it for you?"

"I had to know, to—"

"Know *what*?"

"Keep your shirt on," he said. "I simply had to know what it was like. Years and years I'd wondered: What if you woke up in the morning, so rich you were famous for it, being rich. What if you had your orange juice, read your paper, finished your coffee, all the while knowing that if there was anything to buy you could buy it, any place to go, you could go there, today. Would you make life into a game? Manipulate people like children with an ant farm? What would absolutely limitless means do to your appetites? Would you get a yen for experience per se? Sex? Food? Power? Would you buy only those things—Fabergé eggs, solid-gold putters, first folios, Marie Antoinette's bed and chamber pot, things that other people *couldn't*? Would you try a quiet little murder or two, a little indulgence in *acte gratuit,* just to see if you could get away with it?"

"So?"

"So, I've found out what I wanted to know."

"Which is?"

"Which is that there's nothing much *to* find out. The rich are as bored with themselves as you are, as I am—children, without the imagination of children. That's the thing squelched first, imagination. It's bred out of them as carefully as manners and a taste for pheasant and truffles is bred into them. Then comes distrust—not the distrust a king might have for his courtiers, say; that's expected, the king is the king, the rules are understood . . . the kind of distrust that overtakes people who know themselves only by what other people think of them, or by what they suppose they think. *You've* seen the look. They have it by the time they're eleven years old. A man walking down the street in East Hampton, say . . . he's wearing chino shorts, a blue shirt, espadrilles. A glance, and you know he's worth ten million dollars because he's offering you ten million dollars' worth of training to disguise the fact in the very moment of advertising it. The question in his mind is, do you recognize the deception? That's what his glance your way is heavy with. When he sees that you do, he's had his high for the day. All those glitzy bashes you read about . . . benefits, charity balls . . . rituals, exorcisms to banish the curse of banality. But the thing is, those people aren't monsters. They're just as awful in their little ways as anybody else, as nice as anybody else. They may spend their lives clipping coupons and scouting tax shelters, making marriages that look like closed corporations and all that, but one way or another they build the Taj Mahal and provide for its maintenance. It's only a matter of scale, the same ambitions everyone has, with the difference in visible rewards. Once you catch the signals under the backgammon board, you've caught it all, you know it all."

"But you knew it all, ten years ago."

"Knew it, yes, the way everybody knows. But knowing by seeing, being, *having* it, there's a distinction. One hair's breadth, maybe, but that's what I'm talking about: The hair's breadth difference that will someday give me a book that will rattle teeth like the *Origin of Species*."

"You're not kidding yourself?"

"How so?"

"Kidding yourself that all you're up to is a little research on the reservation? a little fieldwork in the hogans? measuring the last of a Tricker oxford, the thickness of gold on a Coromandel screen, the angle of a Herbert Johnson pinch-front . . . the incidence of bow ties with button-down collars? Thinking that you can take it or leave it, when maybe it's already taken you? Did you ever hear of anyone rattling the pearly gates trying to get *out*? Have you ever heard of anyone close to millions of dollars not his who wasn't corrupted by the smell of them?"

"You give yourself away, pet. In the first place, those gates ain't pearly. They're iron and they work electronically. When you want out, there's a man in the gatehouse named Sidney or Crawford to *bow* you out. In the second place *and* the third place, have I ever been anywhere or done anything that didn't sooner or later turn up between covers? Hardback and paperback? If someone is willing to pay for the cab, why shouldn't I sit back and enjoy the ride? As for corruption, do you think Marcel Proust was corrupted? Sainte-Beuve? Fitzgerald? God, that word. You all use it like a branding iron."

"All who?"

"All you holy keepers of the flame—'a thin talent but an amusing one, at least before it was *corrupted* by its own pretensions'—all these great gifts that are supposed to have been *corrupted* by the demands of the marketplace or the mills of publicity. Or, as one of you put it, 'an all too human craving for sugarcoated trivia' . . . academic *merde* that shows they don't have the faintest idea the way a working writer works. *You* ought to know . . . a writer writes. When you wrote about a friend who just happened to be the hottest thing in poetry since Byron, were you *corrupted?* You had a story to tell and you told it. What's the difference?"

"We're not talking about me. There is a difference . . . some stories you *have,* the way you had the story of little Joel in *Other Voices.* Then there are stories you pur*sue.* From where I sit, and I don't mean me alone, I mean anyone who's watched you come up from Georgia—"

"Alabama."

"—come up from Alabama like, like something unaccountable, like something no one could have guessed was ever *there* . . . From where I sit, you've put all that aside as if it were some kind of mortal embarrassment. Nowadays, instead of creating, you're recording. You created Joel and all the rest of them out of what you hardly knew. They were discoveries . . . for you and for your readers. Now you *know*. There's nothing to discover because it's all there in front of you when you begin. All you can do is move your characters around like chessmen, arrange your observations like furniture in a doll's house."

"There was less imagination in *Other Voices* than you think," he said. "That was a record, too . . . a lot of facts all wrapped up in the gauze of a daydream."

"That may be so, but at least you gave the illusion of distance and the mystery of things. What's going to happen when there's no distance, no possibility of distance—when the life you live is an open book and the only people you know are public figures? How are you going to hide yourself in fame long enough to remind yourself who you are? As far as I can see, you've achieved a reputation at the cost of a career."

"My, my. We do go on. Would you like another drink? Or shall I have them send up a soapbox?"

"I'm sorry. I'll take the drink."

"The thing you can't seem to get through your pretty head is that I've never pretended to be that prose-poet you and the others tried to make me. I have this gift and these resources. With them, I do what I can. They may lead me into the shadow of the House of Usher in one book, and up a lot of creaky stairs . . . in another, they may tempt me to try my own crazy imagination of what someone like Proust sees and what someone like Walter Winchell says. Who's to order me to go on doing what I've *done*? *Other Voices* was my way of finding metaphors for what I knew but couldn't understand. In my big book, I'll do no more, no less. The only difference is that, psychologically speaking, I'm writing from the outside rather than from the inside. I don't have to *find* metaphors to illuminate my ignorance, I have to *make* metaphors that show I can escape the limits of my own imagination, enter into the lives and imaginations of others. It's mimesis, Prof, in case you don't think I don't know my Auerbach, it's making a scale model of the big world that works the way I want it to work. *Other Voices* was my way of shaking myself out of the magnolias, of giving myself up in order to *be* myself. You may not like that, I daresay others won't. But don't put it down to some misuse of God-given talents or corruption of intention or failing powers. You think I'd go frog-sticking without a light?"

Next day we tested the stage at Sanders Theater for reading space and acoustical effects. Later, when a table was rolled into his hotel room, we pulled up our chairs and, formally attired, dined like show-window dummies. "What time is it when you left here last night?"

"About two."

"That's when I went out," he said. "Why didn't you *tell* me Boston was such a lively place?"

An hour later, to a largely undergraduate audience, I spoke my introduction, then watched from the stage as, once more, he set about the task of taking an audience from skepticism to surrender. But the cost was still high, and the task, on this particular evening, was impeded by emanations of malice I'd once been prepared for but no longer expected.

I doubt that the larger part of the audience was aware of a subtle and well-orchestrated attempt to spoil his performance; but I caught wind of it within moments and could tell that T. was also quick to sense its malevolent drift. For reasons never revealed, a number of individuals had bought tickets in widely spaced sections of the theater from which they could coordinate a response to Truman's opening remarks and the first lines of his reading. This took the form of extended and hearty laughter at the mildest of his statements, followed by heavily exaggerated guffawing when what he said was intended merely to amuse. But, just as these crescendos were occurring at ever more frequent intervals, they were foiled, then swamped.

Hitting his stride, Truman sent the crowd into laughter of such genuine delight as to overwhelm the phony outbursts of his persecutors and to reduce what still could be heard from them to scrannel pipings. By intermission, his victory was complete. But when I joined him backstage he was shivering and seemed almost unable to speak. I rubbed his hands, then actually held him to stop his shaking and to lend him some physical warmth. His heart was beating as fast as a bird's. "I'll ask them for a bit more time," I told him.

"No," he said, "I'll be all right, once I get back out there."

And he was.

Barbados, Positano, Berlin—the places to which I lugged my portable Olivetti that year were as far-flung as Truman's. We did not meet until November, when my biography of Gertrude Stein was about to be published and I was in New York for interviews arranged by my publishers to promote it. "Last week," he said when I phoned, "I became thirty-five years old. I think you ought to do something about it . . . like taking me to dinner at The Colony."

The hours we spent there were the soberest with him I could remember. Restless, self-questioning, he spoke only of what he pretended to abhor: the relationship between what the eye observes and what the imagination conceives, between the fact and its resonance, between the truth of history and the truth of philosophy—the whole kit and caboodle of writers' "problems" he had all his life assigned to pedants, or to talents more workaday than his own. What sparked this uncharacteristic inquiry was a conviction that he was "mired" creatively and had somehow to transcend himself. "I have this feeling that I've got to delve and explore," he said, "get out of myself and into something mysterious, do a kind of book that has no precedent."

"No precedent with you, you mean?"

"No precedent with anybody, a way of telling that would give the penumbra of fiction to something as cold as the truth."

This exchange had about it an aura of déjà vu. Challenged to turn a chat into a character portrait, Truman had said much the same thing about his famous interview with Marlon Brando in Japan and later felt that, in *The Muses Are Heard,* he'd turned a reporter's routine assignment into a cunning example of social satire. Somewhere along the line, an idea of a "nonfiction novel" had struck him "like a wave." With it came a conviction that even pedestrian journalism could be mined in search of an art form still to be discovered.

He handed me a clipping, a news service dispatch about the murder of a farmer named Clutter, his wife, and two children somewhere in western Kansas. "When I came across it," he said, "something in me said, 'That's it.' I think I even said it out loud. The point is, how to expand this little footnote to murder into something on the scale of Dostoevski, how to leave myself out of it, assume the omniscient view and make each smidgeon of fact reverberate . . . from blood spots on the stairs to the values of the tribe."

Later that week, en route to the airport and a plane for St. Thomas, I took a letter from my mailbox. "God, what a self-obsessed bore I must have been the other night," wrote Truman. "I still don't know what got into me. Maybe I ought to take to the hills like Jerry Salinger, or get drunk and play Prometheus like Norman, or become a public charge like Carson.

"I once knew a crow who thought she was an Airedale, and it worked, except with Airedales. But all vital signs continue to point to my being me, and taking the consequences. You were sweet to listen and I did love seeing you. While you are bathing away these weeks in the sun, please remember to send kind messages to your cold (but warm) friend."

Confident that Truman could solve any problem he could enunciate, I regarded his sober explorations of old dualities as evidence of a long-delayed brush with metaphysics. At the same time, I knew that soluble "problems" were decoys, that what he was really up against was the conundrum of his existence: He and his fictions, already equals, would soon be one.

Meanwhile, with dedication that often seemed like obsession, Truman began to pursue the grisly facts and elusive meanings of an obscure crime he would bring to the world's attention in *In Cold Blood.* Nothing before had ever so consumed him professionally; and nothing would ever again cause him, for months on end, to trade the lustre and comfort of the life he knew for an existence so rigorous as to seem like a test of will, character, and endurance approaching the asceticism of Simeon Stylites on his pillar. After four years of it—interspersed with spells of working isolation in Spain and Switzerland—he touched down in New York in the spring of 1963. There one day in April, we had a long reminiscent lunch, did our old familiar act at The Poetry Center, and went to still another party.

In the memoir I would eventually write, my report of this occasion was less factual than symbolic—an attempt to show Truman playing Truman in a setting that prefigured his destiny. There is now no reason to obscure the fact that the party was given by Gloria Vanderbilt—long before she began to put her signature on pants and perfumes—or that among the guests were Captain Mainbocher and Diana Vreeland.

> 10:30 P.M. Our hostess greets us at the door of an apartment high over the East River. Not quite "heiress of all the ages" but of at least a sizable chunk of the nineteenth century (shipping and furs) she is wearing blood-red (shoes, gown, mouth) and at her side hovers the most recent of the husbands of aesthetic caliber (a conductor, a

curator, a motion picture director, an author) who have helped her to shoulder the burdens of baronial patrimony.

Since Truman knows everyone assembled in her drawing room, he makes his own way while I am in turn introduced to a visiting couturier from Paris (he made the dress in which Wallis Simpson exchanged vows with the ex-king of England), a lady editor whose imprimatur was essential to the aspirations of trendsetters, two British foreign correspondents assigned to Washington, a banker noted for his collection of cubist canvases of the analytical phase, a woman whose torso is annually designated as Best Dressed, and once more, the logorrheic lady Noël Coward brought to cocktails in Portofino. By the time I can sit down, it's show-and-tell: Truman is passing around Kodachromes of his beach house in Spain, his chalet in Verbier, his dogs, his new car. "Like it?" he asks, and hands me one of an automobile in the shape of a bullet, a silver bullet. Under its half-opened astronaut's roof sits T. himself, at the wheel.

"It looks like something I saw at the World's Fair," I tell him, "the Chicago one."

"Maybe you did. . . . There aren't many others like it. That little buggy is going to take me to Kansas, starting tomorrow morning."

He turns back to the others, resuming a running commentary that is resisted, I note, only by the couturier and the banker, who seem suddenly more interested in the view. Perhaps aware of this, our hostess rises, skeletal in her swirl of bloody chiffon, and bids everyone to follow her into the new bathroom she has designed herself.

Drinks in hand, we trail through a hallway to look into a grotto on the seacoast of Bohemia: multicolored scallop shells, fans of dyed coral, anemones and angelfish, driftwood and echinoids, all the detritus of the littoral zone not quite disguising the fact that the room is a place of ablution and relief.

When we're once more in the drawing room, a slight rumble causes everyone to look up: One wall has disappeared, to reveal four tables set with pink linen and white carnations. At each of them stands a serving man in livery who helps us into our chairs, brings lobster Newburg and champagne, followed by strawberries in little silver dishes.

After supper half of the guests take leave. The rest of us repair to a paneled library, where, over demitasses and liqueurs, discussion turns on the revelations of Beverly Aadland about Errol Flynn; the decline of Sid Caesar and St.-Tropez; Jacqueline Kennedy's trials with wallpaper in the White House; Sonny Whitney's plans for a condominium colony in the Algarve; the affronting vulgarity of Lady Docker's golden Rolls.

Glossy as linoleum, the picture postcard I got from Kansas a month later confirmed Truman's task without indicating the passion that had taken him to a dead box of a motel on the edge of space. In front of it stood an automobile so old it could have been the getaway car for Bonnie and Clyde. Windows reflected blurred images of what I took to be a water tank and a cattle pen. Planted in concrete next to the motel was a road sign: WELCOME TO GARDEN CITY.

"Working hard on my book," said Truman, "and think it is good (so far)."

On leaving Gloria Vanderbilt's that night, we had hailed a taxi that would drop me off at my hotel and carry Truman on to Brooklyn. As we sat back, lumpish in our coats, to rehearse the long evening, I kept from him the fact that my repeated absences from the table and the gathering in the library afterward were caused, first, by a belief I was dying, and then by a dread suspicion I was not. Miss Vanderbilt's bathroom may have had its cretaceous charms, but these were secondary to the exquisite flush of plumbing that swirled my supper away, along with the spongy shreds of my soul. I would one day come to see the humor in waking from a dead faint on designer tiles. At the time, the episode was no more than a private embarrassment touched with presentiment. Within the year I would spend three long terms in Boston hospitals, two of them for major operations.

Truman's note from Garden City—in itself merely the kind of shorthand exchange we were used to, nevertheless signaled the end of that phase of our friendship when my concern for him was lively and, in the relaxation of old intimacy, perhaps seemly. Affection between us had by now survived seventeen sometimes troubled years and, at least on my part, would never diminish. But the ways in which it was sustained had begun to undergo change. Instead of following Truman's career with avuncular concern and anxiety, I simply watched it—often bemused, frequently dismayed, finally appalled.

That note from Kansas arrived on April 22, 1963. Thirty-eight years old, Truman was approaching a boost to his career that would double his fame, quadruple his fortune, and give his pursuit of celebrity unprecedented scope. Eight years older than he, I was in a mood of divestment, soon to be deepened by long hours of hospital-window meditation. What I first wanted to be rid of was ambition, that killer disease whose symptoms were inflated intimations of immortality and whose blight had already made inroads on the particular poetic generation, more or less my own, that it would eventually wipe out. Next was that senseless round of peripheral association known as "the literary life."

For me, it had begun at breakfast tête-à-tête with Theodore Dreiser when I was twenty-two years old and not at all ready to talk to monuments, much less disagree with them. (Dreiser, just back from Europe, had put forward the insanely absurd notion that Hitler and Stalin were about to sign a pact.) Since then, I'd had the heady ups and clay-foot downs of it for twenty-five years, and that was enough . . . at least enough to take me into exile with no curiosity as to what I might be missing.

"Let the day perish, let the day come." My own words were prophetic. Loss of transient acquaintance only deepened my need for friends and made me newly aware of a reservoir of affection long taken for granted. If we are indeed known by the company we keep, who, I asked myself, would bear me witness? I did not have to search for an answer. Without exception, my friends were old friends: those who, more talented than I to begin with and richer in accomplishment, had long ago seen through all of my pretensions, yet had somehow never let me go: Howard Moss, Jean Stafford, Katherine Anne Porter, Richard Wilbur, Elizabeth Bishop.

In the general dismantling upon which I was set, the easiest thing to relinquish was the lure—half financial, half ego-building—of lecture and reading tours. I had sung for my supper in commons rooms, embassies, faculty clubs, and student cafeterias from Pocatello to Copenhagen, Minneapolis to Knokke-le-Zoute, Oxford to Oakland. Then, one snow-capped evening in Salt Lake City, having just missed still another plane, I put my head on the top of an untended check-in desk, delivered a one-line lecture to myself—"Baby, this ain't no way to live"—and fell asleep standing up.

Finally, time had so swiftly transformed New York and London, the cloud-borne cities of my adolescent dreams, that I wandered their familiar streets and squares like a graveyard ghost. Presented with a random snapshot, I could still instantly identify any corner of Manhattan from the Battery to 125th Street. But my old landmarks were gone, all of them, from the Café Brevoort to the Ritz-Carlton to the Apollo Theatre. With them went the days that provided not only the enchantments of Martha Graham, Beatrice Lillie, and Billie Holiday in performance but the chance to see them, talk to them, and, levitated by a touch, come home on air. London, once my idea of civilization and grace beyond reach, was entering that curious phase of self-betrayal in which all of its virtues disappeared into the blare of Carnaby Street, from which they would never quite emerge. An old curmudgeon at the age of forty-six, I wept for time past and vowed to give up city life for good.

So it was that, in the watershed year of 1963, when Truman was in the process of launching himself into space, I was withdrawing— not into myself so much as into a room of my own and a long overdue conservation of energies. Having by then produced ten books, I saw no reason why I might not be capable of turning out a few more. Still deeply devoted to teaching, as I had been for more than twenty years, I had accepted an invitation to take over Robert Lowell's role as a particular professor of poetry at Boston University. My memoir of Dylan Thomas had become the basis of a new play headed for Broadway with Alec Guinness in the leading part. I was looking forward to a summer when I'd reacquaint myself with the inexhaustible charms of Venice and try not to be depressed by the new reality of London; then to a sabbatical winter in St. Thomas where, I hoped, prolonged study of sea and sky might confirm the good sense of my decision to settle down and let go. Above all, I was about to acquire a house on the Massachusetts shore where, for the next twenty years and more, I could at last achieve a lifelong ambition to be, above all, a collector of mornings.

Out of Truman's orbit and committed in spirit to an existence he could think of only as professional and social retreat tantamount to suicide, I went my own way without being aware that among my count of once enchanted and now discarded objects was Truman himself. Across a distance that would never shrink, it was clear that the "offices of friendship" I'd once made so much of would now be his to serve, or to ignore.

As for Truman, the "development" in his career that would lead to new heights of success and a wide reshuffling of his priorities was, of course, the extraordinary publishing phenomenon of his "nonfiction novel," *In Cold Blood.* On its profits he was able to buy an apartment (adjoining that of Johnny Carson) in New York's United Nations Plaza; a small estate with two houses, one for himself, one for Jack Dunphy, in the Hamptons of Long Island; another house in Palm Springs, California, all the while retaining a chalet in Verbier, Switzerland, where much of that book was written.

"Think it is good," Truman had ventured from Kansas, and he was right. The excitement of *In Cold Blood* lies in its immediacy, in the illusion that veils, walls, have fallen away. Readers are engaged in an experience from which it is impossible to withdraw until the last moment has been lived and accounted for. Like Hannah Arendt's *Eichmann in Jerusalem*—its counterpart on a far grander scale of contemporary tragedy—*In Cold Blood* deals with the banality of evil and, in the process, enlarges comprehension without providing answers. Swift-paced, flashing with insight into the minds of murderers and victims alike, the book takes the theme of crime and punishment into a new dimension. If it lacks Dostoevski's haunting gravity, it nevertheless has its own neon-lighted eeriness and Bible Belt grotesquerie.

But the fame of *In Cold Blood* would not for long obscure the fact that it was no lasting contribution to literature—neither in the large account of creative imagination confirmed by succeeding generations of readers nor even in the aspirations expressed by Truman himself. Supposedly a trailblazing start into new territory that was his to explore, the book was actually both the high point and dead end of his career. Thereafter, collected pieces of ephemera, provided with titles and contained between covers, would do no more than mark the time until he was ready to deliver the most heralded masterwork of the century, *Answered Prayers*.

By now a household word, Truman's name was associated no longer with the parochial distinctions of literary assessment but with the hard glitter of success and, soon enough, the careless bravado of self-exploitation. Observing the public figure as it grew ever more into a caricature of itself, I began to surrender to an image that floated, like a Macy's balloon on Thanksgiving Day, over the watching multitude and to lose sight of the man I knew. When two years went by without a signal between us, I felt a certain nostalgia for old times, but with no expectations they would be renewed.

In the mid-sixties, I spent most of another sabbatical winter in St. Thomas. There, to please a friend too shy to speak for himself, I wrote to Truman asking him to give a "special twist" to an inscribed copy of *In Cold Blood*. In the letter, I also included a few remarks about social life on the island. His response from New York came quickly.

"My angel," he wrote, "Life is a mad thing, and getting madder all the time, so this is but a note, lamb chop. The book came, but I can't remember what it is you wanted me to write in it: you and your damned subtlety, see what it gets you? Now write it out for me in so many words! Tell me *exactly* how I should inscribe it. And hurry on home, that place sounds absolutely suicidal. And what are you getting out of it? Stay away from those old dipsos and dissolutes. Anyway, I love you. T."

Made little of then, the note seemed to renew an old rapport and, later, became a matter of sentimental significance in that it reopened a door to the past I believed had been firmly shut. Nine or ten times every year for the next decade, I'd pick up the phone, catch the first syllables of that widely mimicked voice, and be once more in the midst of a conversation that seemed never to have been interrupted.

July 17, 1966 [begins a journal entry]. "Listen," says Truman from New York. "What would you say to the idea that you and I work up a television series?—poets reading and talking about themselves."

"It's been done."

"Everything's been done. So what? I'm thinking of something with a special angle, visually. Remember that old Carl Dreyer movie about Joan of Arc? The one where what's-her-name carries the whole thing in close-ups? The camera stays on her face like a microscope and you get this feeling that just one lifted eyebrow's as full of action as a battle scene."

Intrigued—not so much by the idea as by the fact that it's Truman who's advancing it—I ask what has sparked his interest.

"I was just sitting here, dipping into that anthology you did. Some of those guys are terrific and nobody knows they exist."

"Don't you worry. A lot of people *do.*"

"I detect a note of censure," he says. "Well, old buddy, let me tell you you've got some lulus there, too. *If* I may say so."

"No doubt. What's this sudden interest, Truman? Are *you* writing poetry?"

"Of course. The laureate of the lavatory wall. Look,

think seriously about what I'm saying. All you have to do is say yes. I know the network people to talk to. The thing is, people are beginning to think I'm more involved in criminal justice and prison reform than in literature. I need something public like this to balance out."

"Say I do say yes. What's the next move?"

"No move. Just you sit on your bohunkus until I get the word."

This call, like most of the others—some of which would startle friends who, occupying the place in my absence, would pick up the phone and find themselves being addressed as "lamb chop"—was made to my house in a village of which, in the workings of *piccolo mondo,* I'd first learned from Truman himself.

At lunch in the Plaza's Oak Room one spring day in the late fifties, I had asked him what his plans for the summer were.

"I've taken a house . . . on an island off Massachusetts," he said. "I think I can finish my book there."

"Which island? The Vineyard? Nantucket?"

He shook his head. "I wouldn't be caught dead on either one of them. It has to be a place where I can be alone, not a literary ant farm."

"There *aren't* any other islands off Massachusetts," I said, "unless you mean that string of little ones the Forbes family keeps to itself."

"But there *is,"* he said. "The only people there are some rich Philadelphia hillbillies who come for the summer and guard it like moonshiners—except for this one house I'm getting through a friend."

"What part of Massachusetts is it near?"

"A little absolute noplace called Duxbury. That's where I'll have to go in an outboard . . . for even so much as a paper clip or a can of soup."

Unconvinced, I thought no more about his "little absolute

noplace" until I bought a house there and realized that there *was* another island "off Massachusetts." Across the bay on which my windows looked, Clarks Island was the looming mass of green where, in 1620, the passengers of the *Mayflower* had held their first religious service in the new world and where, in 1958, Truman had served up *Breakfast at Tiffany's*.

Without preface or sequel, T.'s calls sometimes made me wonder if I were merely a sounding board for fleeting notions to which his memory somehow attached me. Hit-and-run as they were, they at least gave a humanizing dimension to stories I read in the papers, especially in those years when reports of mishap and sorry falls from grace began to appear in alarming succession.

"Under the influence and without a license." Simple words on a police blotter would gather irony as Truman's increasing troubles with liquor, automobiles, and controlled substances became staple items for the news services. One of the first of these, according to Truman, was an accident caused by nothing more than the unruly behavior of a dog in the car with him. Whatever the true reason, to learn he'd been pried from the wreckage resulting from collision with a tree on a country road was disturbing enough to warrant a note of concern.

"Dearest M.," he wrote back, "Yes indeed I came very close to being killed and am just now out of the hospital; now just waiting to have the stitches removed. Did you ever get the letter I wrote to Yucatan? or *wherever* it was. I have a house in Palm Springs (of all places!) and wanted you to stop there. It's a lovely house—*if* you like the desert. I will be here until December and would love to see you. T."

In the autumn of 1966, I went to England for research in preparation for some articles commissioned by *Holiday* magazine. My subject was a new superliner the Cunard Company was planning to launch as a replacement for the aging *Queens, Mary* and *Elizabeth.* After visits to Liverpool and Southampton, I settled for a time in London. There, on three occasions of a literary nature, I was dismayed to learn that *In Cold Blood* had become a cause célèbre of a sort that would not have pleased Truman, and might have alarmed him.

From what I could gather, without declaring my "invested" interest in the matter, a prominent drama critic had made accusations which, in the space of a few days, had served to mount a campaign of vilification. In this man's view, Truman had, for cold cash, exploited the young murderers about whom he wrote and not lifted a finger to save them from execution. T. as the hangman's dwarf who, at a signal, jumps on the shoulders of the man on the gallows was not a pretty picture. What disturbed me more were reports that—by some move equivalent to a class action suit—certain individuals were prepared to join together and go to court in an effort to see that British royalties accruing to *In Cold Blood* were confiscated. When I first heard them, these rumors and charges struck me as both gratuitously mischievous and absurdly unreal. When I continued to hear them, they seemed in themselves to have taken on the character of a minor phenomenon. If I could not account for the phenomenon, at least I could alert Truman to the menace, however vague, it represented.

Journal entries made at the time document my ignorance of a social event in New York that resulted in more "coverage" for T. than anything he'd ever written, or would write, and confirm the embarrassment of a letter as ill-timed as it was irrelevant.

November 25.   On foot, to Wigmore Street and the offices of James Gardner, designer of Cunard's new superliner, Q-4 [Later to be christened *Queen Elizabeth 2*]. Half an hour into our talk, he looks at his watch.

"Want to see her? No civilian, so to speak, has ever had that privilege."

Buckling himself into a trench coat, he reaches for a crumpled hat, then leads me downstairs and around the corner to a low-slung roadster with a canvas top. Slithering through traffic, we get to Hampstead in minutes and draw up to a big Edwardian house in a brightly silent neighborhood. To reach his studio, we walk around to the back and down a few steps to a basement door. Flashing a big key ring, he takes a spy's furtive look around the premises, then bids me inside.

"There she is." He nods toward a shrouded shape eight or nine feet long, about two feet wide, with a tumescent bulge in the middle. We keep our coats on while he fixes drinks at a basin with a single spiggot. These in hand, we approach the shape.

"Voilà!" he says, and whips off the shroud.

4:00 Back at the Connaught, order tea, write T.C. re London rumors about *Cold Blood*. Does he know what's/ who's behind them?

"Depending on which masked and bejeweled guest was talking," *Life* magazine later reported, "it was the party of the decade. It was the party of the century, or, plainly, it was the biggest and most glorious bash ever."

November 29. Jet-lagged from the nine-hour flight, rise groggily at five, grope toward the morning papers.

CAPOTE THROWS GIANT PARTY
THE MARVELOUS MASKED BALL—THERE'LL NEVER BE
ANOTHER LIKE IT
ONLY EVERYBODY WHO'S ANYBODY WAS A GUEST
WELL, WERE YOU THERE?

Wincing (Has my letter from London come like a plea? A death's head? A reproach?), I assemble notes for a lecture on Emily Dickinson—The Metaphysics of Domesticity. 10:00 Class in full complement, every shining face. Speak my piece.

December 2.   A phone call takes me from the dinner table.

That voice.

"Hey," I say, trying to get the jump on it, "where *are* you? . . . Out *there?*"

"Maybe somewhere between Jupiter and Mars," says T. "Anyhoo, the party's over and done with, and so am I. It'll take two weeks in Nassau to bring me back . . . to my senses, I mean."

There is a pause, and I am waiting for it.

"I got your letter."

"That's what I was afraid of."

"You do have an exquisite gift for timing, dear heart. I was tempted to call the whole thing off, it would have saved me a lot of money . . . like fifty thousand smackeroos."

At ease, I know he's tracked the convolutions tying me in catatonic knots for days.

"Don't let it bother you," he says, "and don't lose any sleep over that cheap-shot vendetta against me in London. I've been aware of the black hand of Mister Kenneth Tynan for years. What I want to know is: Have you seen Holly Golightly?"*

"A month ago . . . when it opened."

---

* A musical, adapted from *Breakfast at Tiffany's* by Abe Burrows, starring Mary Tyler Moore and Richard Chamberlain. Stumbling toward Broadway, it would collapse there . . . but not before Edward Albee's services as play-doctor had been vainly enlisted.

"What's the poop? . . . in the judgment of your charmed circle?"

"Disaster."

"That seems to be the consensus. Did you by any chance run into Edward Albee in Boston?"

"We had dinner on his last night here."

"You think he's got some crazy big idea how to save it?"

"May be," I say. "We had other things to talk about."

"*F-o-r* instance," says Truman.

Like other of his enthusiasms sparked by new opportunities for self-dramatization, Truman's fantasy of becoming television's impresario of poetry was momentary and, in view of his attitude toward the art of poetry in general, bizarre. For years he'd regarded poets with little more than grudging respect, and there were times when he seemed to regard the work of the best of them as a personal affront. While he seldom read poetry, he could not help reading about it in the same literary journals that allotted handsome amounts of space to the careers of Wilbur, Lowell, Berryman, Roethke, and Bishop, and gave short shrift to his own. At first merely an irritation, this imbalance eventually led him to think what a greater part of the population thought—that contemporary poetry was an arcane if not subversive activity closed to all but initiates. The fact that some of my closest friends were members of this cabal intrigued him. But his curiosity about them had little to do with what they wrote or how they had achieved such obstreperous eminence. What he wanted to know was what they did, particularly in bed.

For the sake of harmony, I'd long since ignored his lèse-majesté contempt for the poets and other writers I admired. Both in private talks and in the public interviews that were rapidly becoming a central feature of his literary life, he seemed to have developed a trick of substituting airy pronunciamento for discussion. Theatrically effective in the beginning, this soon became wearing and, at times, offensive. When, as it seemed to me, his judgments had grown less and less informed and noticeably more coarse and dismissive, I stopped inviting them. Truman could still turn an X-ray eye on people. But it was difficult not to believe that his literary opinions had become blurred in a myopia of dollar signs and that he was interested only in writers whose commercial success rivaled his own.

Daunting but not divisive, these differences were of no significance whatsoever when, by chance, we met on ground where the fame of artists is as negligible as their solvency, and where certification comes solely by the judgment of peers. The occasion was the annual ceremony of the American Academy and Institute of Arts and Letters. Truman already belonged to this august body—as, some day, I would—but in May 1968, my business there was to listen to a citation, accept an award, and take part in rituals I doubted he would have the patience to sit through.

Skipping the noontime cocktail gathering, he did not make himself visible until the luncheon preceding a program scheduled to take place in an adjacent auditorium. Unaware of his presence in the conversational din, I took my seat at an assigned table, and promptly lost my appetite: each of my companions was an enshrined figure I'd been reading and teaching for more than twenty years.

When the main ceremonies of the afternoon were over, I joined a reception taking place under a vast striped tent. Caught up in the flush of the event, I was exchanging chat with Louise Nevelson and Lillian Hellman when I felt a finger pressing into my backbone.

"Congratulations," said Truman. "You want to get the bejesus out of here? I've got a chauffeur waiting. You ought to see my apartment."

His hair was wispy thin, his suit meticulously cut, his tone conspiratorial. I gave him a bear hug.

"Well?"

"I can't," I said. "You come with me instead. There's a supper party midtown . . . I mean, it's being given *for* me."

"What time?"

"As soon as this is over."

"Who was that woman in the floppy hat at your table?"

"Pearl Buck."

"I thought she was dead."

"So did I."

"Who's coming to this supper party that sounds so important?"

"Old friends, some poets. Maybe Albee."

"Watch out. *That* one hasn't drawn a sober breath since he made it into Sardi's. You happy in your house, that village time forgot? I used to wear the skin of my ass out rowing over from the island to send a letter or buy a box of Kleenex. What possessed you?"

"Just a notion that literary life in New York was no life . . . at least not for me."

"All you bunnies scared shitless of competition say the same thing. Come with me, we can talk in the car. I'll send you back to your blessed poets in style."

Tempted for a moment, I let him go on by himself, stayed at my party long enough to witness Edward Albee's eloquent but unsteady pitch for the election of Eugene McCarthy (Edward's interest in alcohol, I learned later, came permanently to a halt after that evening), then sailed downtown in a cab with Virgil Thomson, listening to his deaf-man's monologue on the political naïveté of Arthur Miller and the love life of Mercedes DeAcosta.

Easiest of targets, Truman had been parodied on the Broadway stage since the early fifties, and on television ever since Ernie Kovacs had introduced "Percy Dovetonsils"—a caricature as broad and witless as the name suggests. This occurred in 1952 when television was still "live" and, by coincidence, I was on hand to witness the first public exposure of that mindlessly laborious "creation."

> November 18.   Fly to La Guardia in bright skies, taxi to the CBS studios in good time to collect composure, wit, etc., for an interview with Mike Wallace. Forced to wait about, I watch as someone named Kovacs does a grotesque imitation of T.—limp posturings, fruity lisp, fluttering hands, the whole pansy *shtick*. Strained and unfunny, the performance sags even for the technicians prepared to laugh, fizzles out in silence. Swallowing rage, I grit my teeth and, shunted onto a set consisting of a sham library of fake books, am suddenly "on."

Since then, almost every television comic had taken a crack at Truman, but never without much success beyond echoing the languorous whine of his voice and mimicking his seal-flipper gesticulations. The best parody of Truman remained Truman himself . . . until even he lost control of it. As if goaded into overdoing his own act, he seemed of late to have forgotten the crucial difference between persona and impersonation and so had slipped into self-ridicule.

But if, in public, Truman was becoming the decade's talk show puppet, in private he was still a man with a voice of his own.

> March 7, 1971.   A Sunday morning fire in the grate, Clarks Island invisible in cold mist. On the phone, Truman, spluttering.
> "I'm so mad I could spit," he says.
> "What now?"
> "Tennessee. He's done it once more, under my eyes. . . . Remember little Andrew?—that nice quiet kid used to be social secretary to Mrs. Murray Crane?"
> I listen to a new story which tediously recapitulates a

dozen other instances of promise and betrayal laid at the clay feet of Mr. Williams.

"Dumped!" he says, "like some trussed-up body you'd find in the East River. Meanwhile, the fiend's on the loose, scot-free to do it all over again. And he will. The man's a killer!"

His tale told, Truman regains composure, even manages a bitter laugh.

"You making any money, honey? How do people *live?* I've just been told I owe our beloved government one hundred and ninety thousand dollars in taxes," he says. "Added to that, the Sagaponnack house's in ruins— flooded out like a lean-to shack on the levee."

"What about *Answered Prayers?* Won't that solve everything?"

"That's not my solution," he says, "that's my problem. I've got to live and *re*live it to produce it."

"So what makes it different from any other novel?"

"Just the one inescapable fact that I'm not apt to find the ending until the ending finds *me.* Maybe that's why I get this feeling the book will be posthumous . . . that I've de*signed* it that way."

Early in 1975, I went to Key West—a spot on the edge of my memory as small and far as it is on the map—and there regained the insights and made the connections that would keep me somehow engaged with my old friend until the end of his life. My one previous visit, decades earlier, was brief and—as my journal confirms— not encouraging.

December 28, 1944.   Sick of 23rd Street Beach and Bing Crosby's endless jukebox renditions of "Don't Fence Me In," decide to get the hell away from Miami, if only for the weekend.

Eight o'clock, catch the last Trailways bus for Key West and stand up the whole way, all seats occupied by booze-sodden sailors returning to base. The only hotel, La Concha, is out of rooms but allows me to bunk on a wicker sofa in the lobby.

December 29.   At daybreak, wash up in the men's room, then go out for a long walk on grid-patterned streets. Everywhere, hurricane damage: wind-wrecked street signs swinging on hinges; scattered shards of trash and busted-open bundles of refuse; dead trees on ruptured sidewalks; a thousand reminders of the terrible devastation of spent force.

At breakfast at a diner counter, the man next to me looks like a native. "This hurricane," I ask, "when did it hit?"

"Oh, lemme think," he says, and rubs his cheek. "The big one . . . fifteen, maybe twenty years back."

Continuing, Gulf to Ocean, I come to a stretch of sand piled with sea wrack, strewn with cans and beer bottles. Sitting on an upturned crate, I take off my shoes and watch the milkily vomitous waves roll in. Toes in the sand, bit by bit I feel out the contours of a buried mound of something directly below—until I can see it's the swollen belly of a dead dog.

Back at the hotel, I retrieve my bag, stop for a rum and Coke on Duval Street, and head for the bus depot.

Since then, Key West had stayed in my mind like a sorry condition of the spirit made visible. But memories of its palm-fringed desolation and sunbaked squalor did not prevent me from packing up my typewriter one icy day in March, 1975, and heading for the airport, once more on the spur of the moment and with no idea where I'd lay my head.

A few hours later, I checked into a locally well-advertised hotel called Pier House, unaware that my first choice would prove, in time, to be my last resort.

Situated on the Gulf of Mexico side of town, the hotel was the creation of a Key West native, David Wolkowsky, who had commissioned a Greek architect to build, on the site of the old Havana ferry docks, a structure reminiscent of the famous Habitat of Montreal's Expo '67. Charmed by the hotel's air of venturesome modernity and elegant inefficiency, I studied the big ugly painting by Tennessee Williams that hung in the lobby, wrote my name in the register, carried my bags across a lush and scruffy courtyard, and found my door.

Next morning, setting up shop in my room with a view of passing shrimp boats, I laid out a pile of manuscript to revise, a set of midterm bluebooks to be graded, sharpened my pencils, and, ready for work, changed into shorts and hurried into the sun.

March 4. A clatter of sandals on the Japanese-y bridge between the pool and the restaurant takes me from my book. The noise comes from a chunky figure in khaki shorts who's carrying a grocer's bushel bag and wearing a gray sweatshirt across the front of which is printed: Sonny & Cher.

"Truman!"

He turns, says something sotto voce, and makes his way over.

"What's in that crummy bag?"

"What you expect," he says, "pâté and truffles from Fauchon?"

He sits on the adjoining chaise and kicks off his sandals.

"It's all I could find—my answer to Louis Vuitton. I got here two nights ago, dropped my stuff in this house I rented, went out for dinner, and came back to a total rip-off—two thou or so in cash, all my credit cards, prescriptions, the works."

Half an hour later, heading down Duval Street in the station wagon of a local real estate agent, we're about to be shown a house for sale on a side street near the cemetery with its above-ground crypts. There's a scrubby green lane where two "loaded" Yamahas are parked in tandem, and the house is actually two houses on a quarter-acre plot crowded with gnarled trees, greenery choking on itself, and an empty goldfish pool lined with moss. One house is a barn with amenities; the other, ten feet from the barn's broad door, is a two-story cottage small enough to enchant a dwarf. Other objects in the bosky hideaway are big cork floats with peeling stripes of paint on them, piled-up lobster pots, concrete tables and benches imbedded with mosaics of china and glass. Taking a seat on one of the benches, I contemplate a ceramic frog poised on the lip of the fish pool, a weather-streaked Madonna placed near a big sphere of flaking silver, and wait for Truman to come, shuddering, out of the barn.

"Perfect," he says to the real estate man as they emerge. "I've got enough furniture in Palm Springs to fill every inch of it . . . as soon as I can get rid of my house there."

Spotting me—another gnome in the wilderness of kitsch—he calls out.

"Malcolm, come see!" And we enter a warren of five tiny dark rooms with unpainted walls and a smell of weathering wood. Our inspection, up and down, takes three minutes. Outside, Truman reaches for his checkbook and sits on the stoop to use it.

"For starters, here's twenty-four thousand dollars," he says to the agent, and hands him a check. "There aren't many people around who can do this."

En route back to Pier House, I learn that he's not staying in the hotel proper, but in the trailer with the thatched roof adjoining it. David Wolkowsky had lived there while his hotel was being built and had never got around to dismantling it. Truman's occupancy involved a simple trade-off: for the six weeks he meant to be in Key West, David could have his apartment in United Nations Plaza.

When we meet in the trailer at seven, I find Truman with a stubble-bearded, rugged-looking man of thirty-five or so, dressed in blue jeans and a lumberjack's woolen shirt.

"Meet John O'Shea," says Truman. I've barely withdrawn my handshake when, without a word, O'Shea turns to pour a drink he carries into another room, from which, in a moment, comes blasts of rock music.

"Don't mind that one," says T. "He's having an attack of the mean reds. What brings you to Key West?"

"Spring break. An article to finish. You?"

"Some stories. *Esquire*'s sending an armored car, maybe a helicopter, to pick them up. One of them's actually going to start with a paragraph on the front *cover*, would you believe it?"

Catching up on the time since last we'd met, we hardly need to. Between his out-of-the-blue phone calls and what I've read in the papers there is not much I don't know about the shape of his existence. Still, mindful of the man in the next room, I ask, "Where's Jack in all of this, Truman?"

"Jack's in Switzerland," he says. "When he's not there he's in this little house on the Island next to mine."

The momentary silence is filled by the slow churnings of a shrimp boat approaching a nearby dock.

"But that's not what you mean, is it?"

He drops ice into half a tumbler of vodka.

"Jack's Jack, and he means to keep it that way. His life's

his own. But I think we're better friends now than we ever were."

A blur of recollection makes me squint.

"What kind of a face is *that?*" says Truman. "Can't you believe what I'm saying?"

"Maybe with a little effort."

"Well, Mister Monogamy, let me inform you there are more ways to go—*me!* Remember how I was always humming and singing that old Cole Porter song . . . and *meaning* it?"

"What song?"

"No lover," he sings, *"no lover for me* . . . if you remember the rest of it, it means no *other* lover but the one you've got."

"What made you stop?"

"I found out it was not, as the pedants say, a viable posture. You, for instance. You still under the impression that the sun rises and sets on the same warm body between your no-iron sheets? Grow up. *Toujours l'amour* . . . that Krazy Kat had the right idea all along."

We'll have dinner in the hotel, Truman decides, and excuses himself to dress. In the five minutes or so he's away, the beat of rock is replaced by a monosyllabic dialogue that does not sound happy. "All *right*" are the final words of it, spoken by Truman. When, together, they return to the little cube of a room, O'Shea is still in his jeans and rough-spun shirt, while Truman has changed into an outfit that looks like uncollected laundry—a guayabara hugely oversize, pants of a kind of raw Indian cotton you see in shops specializing in high-fashion sleaze.

Whatever seethes between them is suspended at dinner long enough to allow me to roam across the years at will, Truman to talk, and O'Shea to listen, however sullenly. With no mind to touch upon old points of contention we've rehearsed for nearly thirty years, I can't help feeling that these, after all, are the grit in our relationship, and that neither of us can prevent their reemergence, or even wants to.

What wouldn't T. now give, I wonder, to squelch or eradicate the gossip column items which he not so long ago paid for? How might he explain his embrace of the kind of television celebrity that finds him in situations too degrading to watch? Dare I tell him how often, embarrassed or bored, I've clicked off my set as the same wit that once entranced me now comes packaged in gag lines? These questions remain unspoken and rhetorical. What I most want to learn is the process by which the young devotee of Flaubert and Chekhov has, in middle age, become a walking advertisement for Sonny and Cher. Unable to tax him directly, I begin in left field.

"A long time ago, T., you made what I thought was a useful distinction between a reputation and a career. . . ."

"What was that?"

"You made a point . . . that it was essential to protect your career from the pressures that go with a reputation . . . but that I ought to understand how one can help advance the other. It made some sense at the time. Now I'm not so sure."

"Why not?—didn't I *always* have a reputation that rolled out a red carpet for my career? When the chips were down, what was it but my reputation that could parlay five figures into six? What's so different now? What's changed your mind?"

"Observation. Years on long years I saw Katherine Anne agonizing over the last pages of *Ship of Fools,* forever refusing to write the last page and close the book. The Arabs have a saying, she'd tell me, 'When a house is finished, death walks in.' Her reputation was never out of her mind. 'I don't need any more of it,' she'd say, 'I've had all I could handle from the beginning. God never meant me to write a novel. Why am I doing it? Because my career has shackled me to a contract I made in desperation twenty years ago.' Well, the shackles came off. She produced a book that made a million dollars and lost the reputation she'd basked in for forty years. Overnight."

As I warm to my subject, Truman stares with a kind of dispassionate forbearance.

"I saw Dylan frozen into his reputation, dying of it. 'Once I was lost and proud,' he'd say, 'now I'm found and humble.' His reputation grew and his career shriveled. I saw that a reputation can be more deadly than quicksand."

Truman sits back in his chair, one arm across his watermelon belly, the other cupping his chin.

"Is all this supposed to have something to do with me, Professor?"

"That's for you to say."

O'Shea, who's been more attentive to the comings and goings in the restaurant than to us, suddenly comes into focus.

"That Dean Martin show," he says to Truman. "Hasn't your friend here got a point?"

Ignoring this, T. orders another double vodka without allowing the waiter to remove the one already on the table.

"People think my reputation *is* my career. Let them. Myself, if I had any doubts about the difference I sure as hell learned it those six years I gave to *Cold Blood.* That's the difference I live with, I mean today and tomorrow. God knows, I'm not the sort to confine myself in a cork-lined room to do what I do. But I've got a room like that all the same. I take it with me and hang out the Do Not Disturb sign in five languages."

Music from a steel band that has set itself up on the

sands outside sends the junkanoo rhythms of the Bahamas through the room. Truman, taking a look around, finds himself being waved at by a middle-aged couple seated by the window.

"Friends of mine," he says, excuses himself and leaves the table.

"Did he really buy a house?" asks O'Shea.

Placed on thin ice, I skate for a few silent seconds and do a figure eight. We'd looked at one, I tell him, and otherwise mark time by detailing its least horrifying features, including the ceramic frog.

"The Hirshhorns," says Truman, and pulls out the chair he'd just left. "Joe and Olga . . . big as they come in the art world. I mean, as collectors."

It's after eleven when we adjourn to the bar off the lobby, O'Shea having meanwhile mumbled something to T. and gone off by himself.

"My disco dude," says T., "you ought to see him in action. But he can't help getting himself into fights—fag bashings—usually around three, when only the stray lambs are left."

"Why did he bring up the Dean Martin show? What was behind his interest in that?"

"His way of letting me know he was on your side of the discussion," he says. "Did you see it—the show?"

"No."

"Well . . . it was one of those 'roasts,' when everyone is supposed to put down the honored guest . . . mercilessly, but all in good fun, of course. All I can say is, I've never regretted anything so much in my life. If you'd seen the show, you'd understand why. It took me back to when I was fourteen, everybody's whipping boy and no idea in the world why. Except this time there were millions of people sitting there to watch me turn sick on what I used to gulp down all by myself."

"How come you'd let yourself in for anything like that?"

"I'd seen some of the others—the roasts—and from the outside, at least, they seemed to have limits, some kind of gentleman's agreement about just how far to go, how to hit nerves that might make the subject wince and still not destroy him. Mine didn't, that's all."

When it becomes clear that the memory is making him morose, and even more clear that the nightcap he's invited me to share will not be one but a series, I say good night and go to my room. An hour later the phone rings.

"Know what?" says T. "I went out to find Johnny, hit The Monster and Delmonico's, and came back to find the trailer's been entered, ripped off."

"Of what?"

"Cash money, what else? Not so much as an ashtray out of place, six hundred and fifty smackers *disparu.*"

Late next morning, Truman was methodically doing laps in the pool when I found a place at a table with an umbrella and began to finger the manuscript I was revising. Treading water, he called out, "I *un*bought that house."

Another two laps and he joined me, dripping. "They're giving me my check back."

"How come?"

"It got all mixed up . . . something I don't want to go into . . . between me and Johnny. He came banging in around four. We had it out and made up—in the usual way. Buying that house was one of those lucky moves that clear the air—*exactly* what I had in mind."

"How did you meet John O'Shea in the first place? Who *is* he?"

"My lawyer said I needed a tax accountant. So I said, okay, find me one."

Wrapped in a towel depicting acrobats, he hailed a waitress and asked her to bring us Bloody Marys and hamburgers.

"So, one night, into the apartment comes this bog-trotting Irisher with a briefcase and down we sit, all business. Next night, the same thing—papers spread out, no talk but of what I earned, what I spent, what kind of evidence I'd have to produce to prove it. About *him*, I learned no more than that he lived somewhere in the suburbs with a wife and four kids. He wore this blue suit, black shoes and socks, a tie that looked like the only one he had."

Our Bloody Marys came sprigged out with florettes of celery.

"You can keep this," he said to the waitress. "Bring me one without benefit of the crud, a double."

"So, comes the third night. I know by now he's smart, maybe even intelligent. There he is in these sad-sack accoutrements, and something in me stirs enough to make me wonder what might be under them. Well, Baby Blue, let me tell you I found out. We've been together ever since."

(Ten years later, I would learn from O'Shea himself that they'd met in a place and circumstance having nothing to do with tax returns—a revelation that presented me, posthumously, and for the first time ever, with a falsehood of Truman's exposed.)

"What about the wife?"

"We're buddies . . . maybe more like allies. We talk every day. She's sensible, and fun. The best part is, we both know our man."

Chastened, perhaps, or otherwise returned to his more placid self, "our man" next evening was a new man. The stubble on his beard was gone and he wore a crisp white shirt, fresh jeans, and polished loafers. With his change of costume came a change in perspective. Instead of suffering me as an intruder upon whatever it was I had intruded upon, he looked me in the eye when he spoke and, for the first time, showed toward Truman signs of affection the total absence of which I'd found baffling.

"These fingers are in a permanent clench," he said, and handed me a drink. "I've been typing for six solid hours . . . *Esquire*'s upped the little monster's deadline. The men in black coats are on their way."

"Let him see the manuscript," called Truman from a bedroom. "Malcolm ought to have some idea why I keep you around."

The bundle John handed me was page-by-page flawless. Curious to read at least a snatch of what was being handled like a top-secret document, I'd barely scanned a paragraph when, roseate from his shower and dressed in still another guru's outfit, Truman emerged.

"We've devised a new way to hide money," he said, then spread out his arms and went into a pirouette. "*These* threads sure don't come from Brooks Brothers, *do* they? As I was saying—how to safeguard your moolah. What you do is buy a supply of chicken breasts. Then you place the bills neatly between two of them, like a sandwich, and put them in the freezing compartment. The cash you end up with may be pretty cold, but at least it's still yours."

The restaurant we chose was Key West's most expensive and by all odds its darkest. But candle-lit gloom was not deep enough to conceal the fact that Truman had entered it—neither from the waiter with three glittering rings on his right hand who approved of our selections ("*fab*ulous"), nor from indistinct persons who from time to time emerged with menus, tourist brochures, and blank checks to be autographed.

Bold enough to confront Truman, but too timorous to stay for an instant longer than it took him to write his name, these collectors dispensed with the small attempts at flattery the circumstance seemed to call for and, dead serious, lined up as though they were waiting for visas to be stamped, then returned to their tables.

"There was a time," said T., "when the only thing I'd be asked to

autograph was a book. Now it's everything from gas station receipts
to pricks." He turned to John. "Tell him what happened last night."

"We were at that backyard restaurant at the other end of the
island," O'Shea began, "in a bar upstairs the owners sort of keep to
themselves. The place was jammed with locals . . . maybe what
you'd call the transient locals . . . like Jimmy Kirkwood and Peter
Fonda and the usual clutch of game-fish machos roughing each
other up for the benefit of those English queens down from Sugar
Loaf or wherever it is they live, and things were pretty lively all
round."

"I'll be back when the prologue is over," said Truman, and
headed for the men's room.

"Anyway," said John, "up to our table comes this chick . . . not
bad, but full of gush, who turns around, flips up a miniskirt and asks
Truman to autograph her buns. Not batting an eyelash, he takes out
a felt-tipped pen and scrawls his name across a plump little buttock.
It was funny, really sort of nice. Then, not two minutes later, comes
this kid bartender, Joey they call him, who's obviously been eyeing
the proceedings. The thing is, he's got his jockey shorts in his hand
and not where they should be. One quick cruise and—everybody's
listening now—I turn to Truman. 'You can't sign your name on
that,' I said, 'but maybe you could in*it*ial it."

Back for the punch line, Truman cut through our laughter.

"It's what television does. You know anyone who gets as much
publicity as I do for doing nothing? I used to be famous because I
wrote books. Now I'm famous for being famous. Well . . . maybe I
always was. But these days I don't know, maybe the joke's wearing a
little thin . . . the sense that two people are stepping into any room
I enter . . . one of them me, the other this pop-up illustration that
looks like me and is expected to act accordingly."

An hour later, we were crowded into Captain Tony's, a night spot
where, along with the obligatory stuffed marlin, fading mementos of
Ernest Hemingway provided most of the wall decoration. John had

joined the twenty-year-olds on the dime-size dance floor, leaving us out of the din at the far end of the bar.

"The Old Man and the Sea," said Truman, "what a fake book *that* is. But to get back to what I was saying . . . about fame. Look what it did to old Papa—trapped him in his own armor and made it impossible for him to do anything but pull a trigger. Then even the armor collapsed . . . and the reputation went clattering down with it."

A live band, replacing disco music, made it impossible for us to hear one another. But not for me to catch what a glazed young man in a broken hat was saying into my ear. "So that's ole Truman, huh? Shit . . . right here in ole Cap Tonio's?"

I nodded.

"You ain't shittin' me? I got this ten bucks says that shrimpy l'il guy is ole Capote, ten to one."

Mumbling to himself, he wandered off, Truman none the wiser.

Esquire's "men in black suits" turned out to be one man in seersucker who arrived when he said he would, collected Truman's manuscripts as if they were legal evidence and headed back to the airport. What he carried off in a locked briefcase was indeed evidence. But not, as time would tell, of a kind or consequence then imagined by anyone, least of all Truman.

For nearly twenty years, he had talked to me, and to anyone else within earshot, about his plans for a book on the scale of *A la Recherche du Temps Perdu,* and not dissimilar in subject and substance. *Answered Prayers* he would call it, with a bow to Saint Teresa of Avila ("More tears are shed over answered prayers than unanswered ones") for providing his title. Its subject would be the world of the super rich he'd come to know by intimate association in settings from the Onassian islands of Greece to the jet-set enclaves of *mittel* Europa to Mayfair, Marbella, and on to Lyford Cay, Beverly

Hills, and the guarded precincts of the domain Doris Duke had established in Hawaii. Its intention would be to take down walls, remove masks, and, from a point of close observation, select certain individuals as eponymous representatives of a vast money-powered conspiracy maintained by invisible alliances and a code of behavior permitting the most exquisite refinements of sexual license and ethical squalor.

Just how he was going to handle this ambitious project was never clear, except that, as a variation on the nonfiction novel, the book would eschew the grand designs of James, Proust, and Mann in favor of episodic, perhaps even cinematic, sequences of events that might gain in immediacy what they would lose in structural cohesion. This was entirely consistent with Truman's distaste for exposition, his impatience with the essayistic complement of most novels, and with his confidence that he was on to a new kind of prose in which the techniques of scriptwriting, drama, and documentary journalism might be combined in a work impervious to the line at which fiction and nonfiction meet.

But what had come to puzzle me was the apparent revision in subject matter occurring between our first talks about *Answered Prayers* in the early sixties and his sporadic references to the book in the seventies. In its original conception, *Answered Prayers* was the contemporary equivalent of a Sainte-Beuvean account of a corrupt and licentious society of nobles told by a writer disguised as a court jester with privileged access to scullery, bedchamber, and throne room.

When, ten years or so later, Truman reported he'd been sorting out letters kept for decades, underscoring entries in diaries and journals, and told me—not without a friendly little snort of menace— that "everyone" he'd ever known would sooner or later turn up in the book, I wondered how Barbara Hutton, Lee Radziwill, and Babe Paley might be accommodated—fictionally or nonfictionally—in the same boat with Wystan Auden, Harper Lee, and Mick Jagger.

When there was no further reference to these concerns in our days in Key West, I assumed that Truman was either maintaining the caution essential to work-in-progress, or taking it for granted that I'd read the eloquent interviews he'd given on the subject and had no further curiosity. What he delivered to the emissary from *Esquire* was, by T.'s own account, a packet of short stories. When, to my surprise and perplexity, they appeared in that magazine as excerpts from his novel-to-be, I came to conclusions seriously at variance with what I had been led to believe. The first was that *Answered Prayers* had become a kind of expandable umbrella under which anything he would ever write would somehow find its place. The second was that *Answered Prayers* was, literally, the sustaining fiction of a mind still conceptually alive but imaginatively shriveled, if not moribund.

> March 7, [says my journal] sunlight like claret. It's nearly noon when T. puts down his sunglasses, the new issue of *W,* and peels off his Virginia Woolf T-shirt.
> "You're late."
> "Heavy sex takes time," he says. "Married men are always surprised to find that out."
> He splashes into the pool, roils it end to end, then surfaces.
> "What you reading?"
> I hold up my copy of Brendan Gill's *Here at the New Yorker.*
> "Am I in it?"
> "I'd say, fleetingly."
> "Want to read it to me?"
> " 'In his teens, Capote served for a time as an office boy on *The New Yorker.* He was a tiny, round-faced, slender creature, as exotic as an osprey. . . . Capote dressed with an eccentricity that wasn't to become commonplace among the young for another twenty-five years: I recall him sweeping through the corridors of the magazine in a

black opera cape, his long golden hair falling to his shoulders: an apparition that put one in mind of Oscar Wilde in Nevada, in his velvets and lilies.' "

" 'Long golden hair,' my ass," says Truman. "I was still crew-cut butch and high school conservative. Another piece of the same old shit. You've got a talented queer around, you have to tie him in with Oscar Wilde or some other image of the drag queen 'exotic.' The idea that he just might be a colleague in the same clothes you're wearing, and sweating it out in an office down the hall, is never allowed to cross your mind. Does he have anything to say about *you*?"

"A bit, but not by name."

"What you mean by that?"

"He tells of the night I took Dylan to meet Shirley Jackson and her husband . . . the night the two of them had a romp in the snow. But he doesn't seem to know I was there on the back stoop, holding their mittens."

"Don't let such things bother you. Take the position I take."

"What's that?"

"I don't care what anybody says about me as long as it isn't true."

He disappears into his bubbles and comes up snorting.

"*Esquire*'s paying more than *The New Yorker*," he says. "I mean, paying me more than *The New Yorker would* have."

I wonder: Did he first submit the *Esquire* stories there? Is it conceivable that, after its readership had gobbled up *In Cold Blood* and given the book an unprecedented send-off, *The New Yorker* had decided that the supposed Capote masterwork did not meet its standards?

"They're going to lose a lot of good people if they don't loosen up on their so-called standards," he says. "John Cheever, for one. The story is, he's had it with them, that he's bowed out. They're still blanking out four-letter words . . . in this day and age."

Tempted to assure him that the story's true, as I know from Cheever himself, I watch T. somersault under the diving board and keep my counsel.

"Salinger," he says, and grips the edge of the pool with both hands. "There's another untold story."

"That," I say, "will be number four hundred and twenty, and counting."

"Okay, know-it-all, this is something I witnessed myself."

"So?"

"I had this appointment . . . a private talk with Mr. Shawn. The unusual thing was that when I got to his office I had to wait . . . not five minutes or ten, but close to half an hour. Well, you know how I hate hanging around. I was just about to say stuff it and split when I caught these voices through the wall. I couldn't make out what was being said, but there'd be these sort of sotto voce exchanges, then long silences, then a kind of spastic monologue that went on and on . . . *not* what you'd expect to hear in *that* sanctum sanctorum."

As he speaks, two women of seventy or so, identical twins, claim adjacent chaises, put down towels, puffy little reticules cinched by what look like napkin rings, and sit, side by side, dangling their feet in the pool. Gaunt as crows, with aquiline noses and pepper-and-salt hair cropped to the bone, they wear black bathing suits composed of tank tops and close-fitting knickers, and seem to share an eerie mechanical impulse that makes them move uncannily in unison. When one of them turns her head or lifts her hand, so does the other, instantaneously. Astonished, I keep one eye on them and one on T., who's unaware of their presence.

"So there I sat," he says, "cooling my heels, wondering

who in the name of heaven was going to open that door. What do you know? Out comes Jerry, big as life, tears running down his face. Two strides and he's away. Never even saw me."

Four eyes glittering, the twins observe Truman, neither moving a muscle.

Out of the pool, he towels himself down, reaches for his glasses, puts them on, and pinches the back of my neck.

"Mother . . . of . . . God," he says.

Oblivious, the twins have shifted their single gaze to a passing gull.

"If only Diane Arbus were here."

1.00. Lunch on the waterside deck with Janet Aaron and Madeline Fisher. Afterward, passing the little Chart House bar off the lobby, I'm stopped by a rapping on the window. T. beckons me inside.

"Good news," he says, "I'm getting my little black bag back—credit cards, pills, everything except the cash."

"Where was it found?"

"Where else?—at the police station. Johnny's been convinced it was there all along. So, this morning, he bore down. If the bag wasn't produced in twenty-four hours, he told them, *Mister* Capote would tell his impressions of Key West next time he was on the Johnny Carson show and give the place the biggest black eye since the hurricane of '37. They said they'd take another look, ha ha, at their pile of unclaimed items. And, of course, there it was."

In a few minutes, John arrives, to escort him to police headquarters. With a plane to catch at three, I go along with them as far as the parking lot to say good-bye.

"We'll miss you, baby face," says T., and gives me a

hug. "Don't you ever again believe anything you don't hear from *me.*"

Moist-eyed, I watch them go—two lumpish figures in the blazing sun, one ambling ahead like a mother duck, one waddling behind in his guru bloomers.

God bless them, I think, if only Diane Arbus. . . .

A year later, *Esquire* published Truman's "Unspoiled Monsters." Supposedly a section of *Answered Prayers,* this head-hunting safari into the wilds of his youth and mine combines fact and fiction with a wicked but unsteady hand. The fictive parts of it, transparently "made up," are so strident as to border on situation-comedy slapstick. The most imaginative moments in the piece are the side-stepping turns and evasions by which Truman reshapes people and occasions long familiar to me and to anyone else who came to Manhattan literary life when he did. But "Unspoiled Monsters" covered so much of the ground he had geographically and figuratively traveled that I wondered what might still be left to tell.

Resources and strategies. Truman had an ample supply of both, and knew when to use them. But this conviction was reassuring only to a point. Beyond it was a puzzle—the malevolent glee of "P. B. Jones," (the alter ego T. had chosen) as he reduces his extraordinary life to a peep show and inevitably turns his readers into eavesdroppers and voyeurs. What had possessed Truman to transform the dear dead friends of our salad days into pseudonymous grotesques? Was there, even on his own terms, even one among them more open to contumely and censure than himself? What had generated such indiscriminate bitterness? Misconceiving the liberating nature of disgust, had he settled for gratuitous malice?

Instinctively, and absurdly, concerned to "protect" my friend, even from himself, I began to cast about for means of countering comments I'd have to swallow or oppose, then came abruptly to my senses. Any attempt to "save" the Truman I cherished and loved would be embarrassingly naïve in intention and superfluous in effect. On the cover of *Esquire*—costumed in total, if not basic, black— there he was, the world's self-appointed tribune. Lightly fingering a stiletto, he peers from the brim of an ominous black hat with an eye as blank and lethal as a cobra's.

Studying this calculated playacting, however childish, I found it difficult not to believe that, in merry pursuit of "monsters," Truman had himself joined the count of his own fair game.

By this time, his Sunday morning calls to Duxbury had become less frequent, and tended to take the form of monologues without a discernible point. "That's my boy!" he'd say by way of complimenting me on some poem of mine in *The New Yorker* or a review in *The New Republic* or the *Times*. But these little salutations de rigueur were merely preludes to notions on his mind or chitchat assuring me that, no matter what I'd read or heard, his life was rich in romantic interest and that he was wholly in control of his destiny. His chitchat had a certain entertainment value: he was going to "mount a campaign" to make Jane Bowles famous; he'd arrived at a "final decision" to buy an antebellum home for his retirement in Mobile, Alabama; Janet Flanner was his candidate for beatification on the road to sainthood; Yoko Ono should be recognized as "a blight on the landscape."

But to hear, repeatedly, that he'd "sent packing" this or that individual who'd turned up in his life became of no more concern to me than his announcements that it was raining hard in New York, or that, hungry for Oysters Rockefeller, he was about to "sally" toward lunch in the Oak Room.

Toward the end of the seventies, these calls ceased—either because I was not at home to receive them, or because they were never made. Truman was once more "out there," perhaps "between Jupiter and Mars," but in any case on the year-long ride that sixty thousand dollars' worth of cocaine kept in orbit. As I'd soon learn, he was also between hospitals and drying-out clinics, and between intervals of rehabilitation and episodes of incontinent squalor beyond the worst deprivations of grace he had himself ever described or imagined.

Meanwhile, notes of encouragement and affection I addressed to him lay untouched among accumulations of mail he did not bother to open for months on end. Phone calls to his unlisted numbers went unanswered.

"Don't give up on me," Truman had once said, "I mean, don't give me up." Time, I thought, had finally done what I could not. But not quite.

The handwriting on the Xeroxed copy of a postcard I took from my mailbox one summer morning was unmistakably Truman's, its message a curt statement to the effect that he had authorized a man named Gerald Clarke to undertake a biography and that he and Clarke would appreciate my "frank" cooperation.

Uncertain as to the full implications of what "frank" might encompass, I pondered the note for a while, then sent off one of my own asking to be reassured as to the degree of candor he would consider permissible. His response was the last few words of a correspondence maintained for more than thirty years.

"Dear Heart—," he wrote, "G. Clarke is a very good writer and v. nice. You will like him. Tell him whatever you want—God knows everyone else has. I've lost 35 pounds, had a million dollars worth of dental work and now look 16. Love—T."

There would also be two more phone calls before my connection with Truman went dead. The second of these, an invitation—conceivably a plea—to join him in Miami Beach came from T. himself; the first came from John O'Shea who, in 1977, still held to the belief that, even in extremity, Truman might "listen to reason."

O'Shea's call, for reasons he could never have guessed, was inopportune: my bags were packed for a trip by sea through the Panama

Canal to San Francisco and—as a journal entry reveals—my mind was preoccupied with the sudden loss of a friend of more than thirty years.

September 13. Up before dawn, try to "take in" Helen Vendler's call: Cal Lowell dead in a taxi en route from Kennedy to Elizabeth Hardwick's. Heart attack? Stroke? No matter. Gutted in a moment, the years between glisten like a boneyard.

Late morning, Holly Stevens on the phone. She's booked a cabin, will make the trip with me. "We're due in the Gulf of Tehuantepec on Dad's ninety-eighth birthday," she says. " 'A Sea Surface Full of Clouds'—we'll have a ceremony. Maybe at sunrise."

Other calls: the Wilburs stunned, Elizabeth Bishop desolated. "Two weeks ago he proposed coming over to North Haven," she says. "I told him 'some other time.' Now there is no other time."

Resigned to a day of postmortems, I pick up the phone once more.

"Malcolm? John O'Shea here . . . the name mean anything? Key West? Truman?"

"Johnny!"

"I'm calling from Santa Monica. Can you give me two minutes—to say what's on my mind?"

"Take your time."

"It's this. Truman's in Smithers . . . that drying-out place in New York . . . the same one John Cheever was in a couple of years back."

"I know."

"Well . . . the medicos there have found out that T.'s been on amphetamines that someone's been smuggling in, and they're going to let him go. The poor bastard's last chance, and he's blowing it, the same way he blew it here . . . when everyone in the A.A. group we went to knew he was on the sauce but me. Well, put that out of your mind the way I have. The fact right now is that I talk to him every day and it does no good. I can't get through to him. Someone else has to, someone he trusts. What I'm getting at is: would you go to see him?"

"God help us, Johnny, why would he have any reason to trust *me?*"

"Because you're the only one in sight who doesn't bullshit him. Listen, I've known T. for five years now. All he's got left are hangers-on and users—dumb groupies who don't know a metaphor from a lawn mower. It has to be someone from where *he* comes from, someone who can level with him, and maybe vice versa."

I explain my situation: passage booked, bags packed, etc.

"If you can't do it," says O'Shea, "what about John Cheever? I've been told it was you who got him into Smithers and saved his life."

"Hold *on,* Johnny. Cheever* saved his own life. I tried to see him through a bad time. That's al!."

"Is there some way you can get him to see Truman?"

"I can try."

"Now? Today?"

"Give me half an hour. I'll call you back."

I dial Ossining, reach Cheever himself.

"Give me two minutes to explain my business," I tell him.

"Take your time."

I do.

When I'm finished, there's a moment of silence.

"The signs are not good," he says. "Smithers expects

---

* Except for a letter from Cheever in which he'd characterized his recovery as a religious conversion following upon his decision not to die "an obscene death," I'd not been in touch with him for more than a year.

cooperation—at least, acquiescence—to what they try to do. You aware that I've never met Capote?"

"I am . . . and so is Truman. He wonders about you."

"So do I," he says. "But I guess that's beside the point. Tell O'Shea to call me and I'll see what's possible. Anytime, tell him, except between eight and ten."

A little snort of laughter, quickly stifled.

"My evenings belong to A.A."

Back from California, I found a letter from O'Shea acquainting me with the critical pass to which matters between him and Truman had come. Truman would soon be released from Smithers, "probably on November 12 or so," he wrote. "As far as I know, he has been 'detoxed,' and has 'kicked' both booze and pills. . . . When I sent T. off to New York, I told him I'd be here when he returned. I was certain that I would not. But, in the face of suicide threats, etc., I had no choice but to tell him that."

Meanwhile, he'd written to Truman making clear the fact that he would not be there, without saying where he would be.

"I have guilt about 'abandoning' him, irrational, emotional," his letter continued, "but I think, in the long run, this will prove to be a solution for Truman, as well as for me. . . . If, indeed, there is a solution. He knows the 'mechanics' of A.A. . . . and if he will acquire, or even assume, the humility to do what is asked of him—namely, go to meetings, call sober people, don't drink one day at a time—he has a chance to live again. Or he'll die.

"On a gut level, I need time for myself. I went from having a wife and four children dependent upon me to the exalting position of being, aberrationally, depended on by Truman. . . . It is time for the boy who was programmed to be the Irish Catholic husband father civil service Church-going zombie to crawl into his cave of selfhood and sort out—what I want out of the dwindling time left.

"Though I've told Truman that I'm going off 'somewhere,' all I've done is change my telephone number to an unlisted one. I have a sense of you as being totally honest, so I'm assuming you will keep this information from T. and others who might relay it."

Not long after his release from Smithers, Truman came into the most widely publicized of his troubles—unceremonious removal from the stage of a college auditorium in Maryland. As the papers reported the incident, Truman was drunk, incoherent, and careless enough with his language to be judged obscene.

I read this story and others like it soon to follow with a despair to which I'd long been inured, yet with a twinge of affordable guilt. As a letter from O'Shea retrospectively indicates, Truman had persisted in the belief that he could still outwit those around him.

"Evidently," wrote O'Shea, "he had while still at Smithers arranged a college tour. A.A. suggests 90 meetings in the first 90 days of sobriety. Anyone planning a college tour in the first 30 days of sobriety obviously had very little commitment.

"In early '77 I had no desire to resume with T. Through the persistence of Joanne Carson I agreed to talk to him. After a while. I continually told him No! No! No! He was drinking, he was using. I was clean. He kept insisting that he wanted to 'clean up.' Carson, whom I'd told repeatedly that I'd had it with his empty promises and his repeated abandonment of me (Palm Springs in '74, Key West in '75, Malibu in '76—K.W. perhaps slightly justified) proposed first to me and then to him: A *gift* of money, an irrevocable gift against the possibility of his again abandoning me.

"He came. I put the money in a C.D. After a week of sobriety on his part I promised that a year later I'd treat him to a tour gastronomique of Europe. He'd be sober a year then, I'd be sober almost 2½ years.

"I took him to A.A. meetings daily. My sponsor was a sober alcoholic doctor who treated T. for liver problems and who gently tried to convince him to get off downers . . . to no avail. An article of dogma in A.A. is that pills will *always* lead back to booze. I told T. that after he had 90 days sober, we'd begin working on the drugs. That was a half way measure for which I've always had regret. We set up housekeeping in an apartment in Santa Monica. An actor in one instance, and an actress a week later, told me at meetings that they didn't think that I should take T. to meetings while he still drank. I was blithely unaware that he did. But, he was drinking. I confronted him. He ran off to Carson's."

Seven years later, he would once more run "off to Carson's," and never return.

In 1978 I resigned my professorship and, in the giddiness of release from thirty-six years of teaching, bought Crown House, the stately St. Thomas home of the original Danish governors of the Virgin Islands. There one bright December morning, I rose early, listened to the raucous talk of some resident green parrots, watched clouds under which the island seemed to sail, and sat down at a dining table big enough to accommodate nine other persons. Alone in a setting where mahogany and crystal chided my excursion into *folie de grandeur,* I wondered: Who might they be? From the shadows of a lifetime, who would emerge to keep me company?

Thinking about them, I began to write about them and—with the assistance of journals kept for thirty-five years—to fix them in the times and places about which memory alone is by nature careless. Resurrected to fill my table and to entertain my isolation, nine figures were eventually reduced to six in a series of memoirs not unlike Truman's own "conversational portraits," and published as a book.

Begun in St. Thomas, this volume was completed in the second of my summers in Venice, where (as journal entries from 1979 indicate) Truman was the object of contention in one quarter, of nostalgia in another.

> July 4.   Leo Lerman's luncheon party on the Gritti terrace—his gesture to patriotism and his salute to Peggy Guggenheim who, he tells me, will be glad to have me

escort her back to the Palazzo Venier de Leoni. My place card puts me between the Baronessa Maria Teresa Rubin de Cervin and Susan Sontag. Seating myself, I greet them both, then turn to Ms. Sontag,* noting with some surprise the ebony richness of her hair and its trademark streak of white.

"Lewis Wharf in Boston to the Gritti," I remind her. "Aren't you a walking miracle?"

"The miracle's in Paris," she says, "the doctors I found there."

Since the table is too large to allow for general conversation, noisy water traffic too close, we are left to ourselves. In the course of chat, we get onto the two literary lawsuits of the moment: Lillian Hellman's against Mary McCarthy, Gore Vidal's against Truman. Dismayed by both, I say what I think and invite Ms. S. to do the same.

"Forget the issues," she says. "Writers should *not* sue writers."

Midafternoon, I assist Peggy Guggenheim into the *traghetto* plying between the pavement by the Gritti entrance and the Dorsoduro. Once across the Canal, we continue on foot and keep to the slow pace her health demands. At the last little bridge before the gate to her palazzo, we stop to rest.

"Truman never comes to see me anymore," she says, "doesn't seem even to come to Venice. Do you know why?"

I think: Has she not read his devastating description of her in "Unspoiled Monsters"?

"The trips he takes these days are closer to home," I tell

---

* I'd last encountered her two years earlier, at the impromptu gathering in Elizabeth Bishop's apartment following funeral services for Robert Lowell. There, I'd learned from her of the battle with cancer she'd been waging and of the chemotherapy that had rendered her all but bald.

"How did you handle that?" I asked.

"Wore funny hats," she said.

her, and bite my tongue, just as we're approached by a disheveled couple in a hurry.

"Pardon me, ma'am," says the large and sweaty husband. "How do we get to this Guggenheim museum of art?"

"Straight ahead," says Peggy. "You can see the gate from here."

Charging on, he calls back. "Thank you, ma'am. We're from Little Rock!"

Aren't we all, I say to myself, and take Miss G.'s arm.

August 2.   On the vaporetto, Gore Vidal; both of us, we learn at once, en route to cocktails with Sheila, the hard-mouthed Duchess of Bronte.

"What's all this about you bringing suit against Truman for a million dollars?"

"He's a liar," says Vidal. "Someone has to have the guts to shut him up."

"I've known him for thirty-three years," I tell him. "Not once have I caught him in a lie."

"That only tells something about you," he says. "He even lies to himself. That book of his, *Answered Prayers* . . . outside those few crappy pieces of gossip in *Esquire,* it doesn't exist, never did."

"That may be," I tell him. "I still don't think writers should sue writers."

"You got *that* shit from Susan Sontag, right?"

Disembarking at the Rialto, we make our way through crowded *passaggetti* to the Duchess's and are stopped there by the yipping of a feisty little terrier guarding the courtyard.

Out comes Sheila herself.

"Fuck off, Iago," she says, and greets us with cold kisses.

Halfway into the party, Gore taps my shoulder.

"Meet me at the Gritti," he says. "Ten o'clock. We'll talk it out."

10 P.M. The Gritti terrace. Gore with Barbara Epstein.

"Can you tell me what it is," I ask, "that makes Truman think you have some mysterious obsession about him?"

"Truman thinks *ev*eryone has an obsession about him. *Him*—a dumpy little lowbrow forever peddling the one thing he's got—a public relations campaign masquerading as a career. You ever heard him express one idea you wouldn't expect to hear from a housewife on some back porch in Kansas?"

To "talk it out" is but to confirm intransigence, I can see; and so does Mrs. Epstein, who, excusing herself, soon leaves us to what turns out to be a gentle exchange of reminiscence.

Each in its own way, these fortuitous reminders of Truman were intriguing. But they had little pertinence to the young man I was intent on recapturing for myself when, each morning before dawn, I'd flick on the lamps of the Palazzo Barbaro and find my way to the library where the ghost of Henry James was my faithful companion and the tidal wash of the Canal below my musical accompaniment. Early in October, I closed its windows on the long summer and packed my memoirs into a bag I carried to Boston. Since Truman was the subject of one of them, it was essential to have his permission to quote from letters I'd kept and to have his approval of what I intended to publish. The problem was, first, how to reach him at some point of sobriety in his peripatetic life, then how to gain his attention long enough to secure his sanction, if not his imprimatur.

Just as I'd begun to devise ways of finding him, he found me; but in a circumstance of no benefit to either of us.

Arriving from Key West on a winter visit to Boston, I picked up a memorandum two days old: "T. Capote phoned from Florida. Says wld. you join him there as soon as possible." Accompanying the message was a number I recognized as being within the Miami exchange. I dialed at once, only to be informed by an operator that the number had been disconnected.

Puzzled on one score, defeated on another, I persisted with increasingly dispirited efforts to catch a broken butterfly of no known habitat. Months of inquiry went unrewarded. Lacking any kind of response, my only alternative was to surrender the task to others more closely acquainted with the orbit in which he moved. Through a grapevine transmission of his whereabouts involving lawyers, agents, publishers, he was found and accosted, appropriately enough, in the swimming pool of a Long Island friend. Within the week, I had in hand what I'd for so long sought: "Re: John Malcolm Brinnin. Yes, Mr. Brinnin can write and publish anything about me he cares to. Truman Capote June 11, 1981 Bridgehampton, N.Y."

And so I did—chilled by the impersonality of the document, disappointed not to have had the advantage of that gift of total recall which, according to Truman, was the magical factor in the thrust of his nonfiction writings, yet pleased to have been granted so broad a license.

When *Sextet* was published in 1981, I was in for two surprises. The first was scores of letters from readers who saw my Capote memoir as an attempt to rehabilitate a fading reputation and who were impelled to confess that, disaffected by "what had become of" the young Truman, they had regained perspective and, with it, sympathy. The second was the response of Truman himself: silence.

Unable to interpret this, I made uneasy assumptions. These ranged from the possibility that he had not read the book to the not unlikely possibility that "another item about yours truly" had finally become anathema. Nothing obscured the simple fact that "my" Truman may have been a revealed delight to strangers but that to the subject himself, it was a portrait of no consequence.

Months went by before I came upon an opportunity to learn the truth . . . in the course of a Duxbury visit from a gentle friend and neighbor of Truman's who shared his confidence and whom I knew as a man incapable of dissembling. When, point-blank, I asked him how Truman had "taken" my account of him, he answered as directly: "He thinks it's well done, but says it's inaccurate."

How true this may be, I'll never know, since Truman alone could have put straight what memory may have distorted. There was nothing to do but accept this report as final and trust that most readers would continue to regard the memoir as the fond recollection and tribute it was meant to be. This they did, with an outpour of feeling that sustained a shriveled heart, and might have warmed Truman's.

But the last word would still be his.

When a compilation of interviews with him was published six months after his death, my memoir—largely this memoir—was introduced as a point of discussion.

"How well did you know John Malcolm Brinnin?" asked the interviewer.

"He's never been a close friend of mine," said Truman, "he never really *was* a close friend of mine."

Not easy to absorb, much less to explain, his statement must nevertheless be honored. To it, I have no answer but these pages, no response but, blessing Truman's handful of ashes, to quote a forgotten sage: "Thou knowest this man's fall, but thou knowest not his wrastling, which, perchance, was such that his very fall is justified and accepted of God."

ACKNOWLEDGMENTS

For contributions to my knowledge and understanding of events beyond the limited compass of this memoir, I am indebted to Gerald Clarke, John Hohnsbeen, John Matthew O'Shea, David Wolkowsky.

Ben Belitt refreshed my memory of the wording of the passage from Dorotheus ending my story.

For suggestions that helped bring cohesion to scatterings of memorabilia, I am grateful for the editorial skills of Merloyd Lawrence.

J.M.B.

INDEX